Joyce Stranger was born in London but has always lived with animals and taken a keen interest in wild life. She started writing at a very early age and is now the author of bestselling novels, mainly based on her own experiences with animals; and of an equal number of children's books, one of which, *Jason*, has been filmed by Disney. *Two for Joy* follows the highly successful *Two's Company* (about Janus and Puma) and *Three's A Pack* (about Janus, Puma and Chita).

Joyce Stranger and her husband live in a 300-year-old cottage in Anglesey. They have three children, one an electronics engineer, one a vet and one a zoologist; and they have five grandchildren and four step-grandchildren.

Also by Joyce Stranger

THE STALLION
REX
CASEY
RUSTY
ZARA
FLASH
KYM
THE RUNNING FOXES
NEVER COUNT APPLES
NEVER TELL A SECRET
TWO'S COMPANY
A WALK IN THE DARK
THE JANUARY QUEEN
CHIA THE WILDCAT
ONE FOR SORROW
KHAZAN
A DOG CALLED GELERT
LAKELAND VET
WALK A LONELY ROAD
THE MONASTERY CAT AND OTHER ANIMALS
HOW TO OWN A SENSIBLE DOG

and published by Corgi Books

Two for Joy

Joyce Stranger

CORGI BOOKS

TWO FOR JOY
A CORGI BOOK 0 552 12525 3

Originally published in Great Britain by
Michael Joseph Limited

PRINTING HISTORY

Michael Joseph edition published 1982
Corgi edition published 1984

This book is set in 10/11 Palatino

Corgi Books are published by
Transworld Publishers Ltd.,
Century House, 61-63 Uxbridge Road,
Ealing, London W5 5SA

Made and printed in Great Britain by
Hunt Barnard Printing Ltd., Aylesbury, Bucks.

List of Illustrations

The author would like to thank Seán Hagerty for supplying the photographs

Chapter One

People are always asking me why I write about animals and how I do my research.

The answer to both is the same.

I live with animals and I don't do any research as such; I just watch what happens and write about the way I live. Much of the time I am with my dogs, so I write about them, these days, as that is autobiographical.

I am sitting now at my desk. If I lift my eyes I look up to the horizon of hedges and sky; there is one house only visible, half hidden by trees; a typical greystone Welsh cottage, its roof of slate, covered in moss. Apart from that I am looking at fields and copses, at the banks of the tiny river, where the heron often stands, at drystone walls, at a large flock of sheep, most of them lying quietly; two are feeding. Scattered among them are the newly calved cows, separated from the main herd; a Friesian, a Charollais cross, probably crossed with a Friesian; a little calf whose white face and black body proclaim him a Friesian–Hereford cross. That white face in the Hereford comes out always in the crossbred calves, giving them a very odd appearance at times; there is now a little one, born the night before last, that looks as if it is a pedigree Hereford.

If I walk up to our post-box, over two hundred yards away from the house, fixed by the gate that leads to the lane, the cows in the next field will be pushing their noses into the hedge and the dogs will be sniffing back at them. The lane is so narrow that driving down it is like pushing a stopper into a bottle; no car can pass. We have to reverse round narrow bends to let others through; or they have to back out and let us by. When the cattle are loaded into the truck to go to market, our neighbour 'phones to warn us

7

that the lane will be blocked for an hour or so.

There are no pavements in the village street; there are only three shops, one of which is a post office; eight hundred people live in our village.

Our back garden is outside my window; a narrow strip of mown grass; beyond it is the asparagus bed and then the French beans, almost over, as summer is dying and autumn is just round the corner; beyond that is the patch where I train Chita, my now four-year-old German Shepherd bitch (or Alsatian as they are more often known). Her scale is there, an upright affair consisting of removable boards that slot into two posts and are built up to six feet; ready for competition Working Trials. There is her hurdle and the long-jump which will extend to nine feet. Our daily routine is started on that patch of grass. In the afternoons we may be out by the beach, Chita practising walking beside me without racing after other dogs and terrifying them, or chasing seagulls; or in the fields, learning to follow a trail laid by me or by one of my friends, over grass, or plough, or stubble. She has come a very long way indeed since I first wrote about her in *Three's A Pack*. I am very glad I recorded her early days. Letters from readers come in quantity to prove how much a book like that was needed by those who buy dogs as pets. The file bulges.

Yesterday afternoon was fine, so we tracked on plough. We do not have empty fields for very long; there may be hay, or crops, or potatoes; in the grass fields we have sheep or cattle. All the space is used; when a field is ploughed we have only a few days to practise before something else is sown and the field is taboo again. Few farmers let people train on growing crops, though this year at Ellesmere dogs had to search and track in waist-high wheat. Few could cope. They had not had practice.

Out in the sunshine, I place my marker poles along the dark newly turned earth, with Chita tied to the telegraph-pole watching me, as ploughland is new to her; if she were more experienced she would stay in the car and be brought out an hour later to trace the path where I had walked. Now she watches so that she understands that here, on earth, instead of on grass, her nose must lead her along my track.

I pinpoint a telegraph-pole with a chimney behind it and walk a line to those, counting my paces, dropping the articles I want her to find; at this stage a 'mouse' made of fur, and a ball sewn tightly into an old glove, so that if I throw it and she catches it, she can't swallow it, as some dogs have. Balls need to be too large to go to the back of the dog's mouth.

She tracks eagerly and fast and on this uneven ground it is difficult to hold her back at a pace that I can manage, without stumbling or falling into the mud. She finds 'mouse' and mouths him, and drops him; she wants to know where the track goes, not what is on it; she has shown me that she recognized the 'mouse' and I pick it up, encourage her, and we go on till we reach the gloved ball and she is ready for a game and high praise, knowing she has done well and reached her objective. When I lay her tracks, or when Lesley lays them for me, the gloved ball or some other reward is always there at the end of the line, or she will wonder why we have to track out purposelessly; this way, she is due to find a trophy and the idea becomes embedded firmly in her mind. There is point to the exercise.

I wrote in *Two's Company* about my two most recent dogs; Janus and Puma. In *Three's A Pack* I wrote about the little monkey that I bought after them hoping to teach her the necessary knowledge for competing in Working Trials.

That book told the story of her life for the first eighteen months from being an impossible puppy, right from the start, from the moment I got her, through the gradual teaching that turned her into a very rewarding dog indeed. I was going to wait until I had gained at least one Working Trials qualification for her, but a number of people have written to me to ask me why there is not yet a sequel as Chita is now four; and Sheila Alcock, who writes a very interesting regular column in *Our Dogs*, made me realize in a letter

9

to me that in fact I do have another book, as this is an exceptionally interesting dog. How interesting even I had not appreciated, at first.

I have also discovered from readers' letters that Chita is far from unique in some ways; though she is in others, as she is very tough indeed in her attitude to training and to pain. She does not notice injuries, which makes it hard to keep her from aggravating them, as she hates resting; and a lame shoulder, due to hurtling at top speed into a tree when she was running free, must be rested.

The letters in my files are fascinating to reread. The first came long ago from the editor of the *Alsatian League* magazine asking me if I would write articles on her, giving a month-by-month account of her progress. That is followed by letters from readers of the articles saying how interesting and helpful they were. I stopped writing them when she was no longer a pup as they were titled 'Pup's Progress'. There is a letter from a reader who read the book to her children; they adored it and the naughtier Chita was the more they enjoyed her antics; children would! I did not always enjoy the mayhem she managed to create.

There are letters from some breeders commenting on her and on how useful the book is as it shows up points that those who sell puppies do not always appreciate; often breeders keep dogs in kennels and don't realize that those of us who have pets in the house expect far higher standards of behaviour. We can't push them outside. Some owners don't know how to train the dog to get superb house manners. Much 'cruelty' by first-time owners is not such in fact but is due to lack of knowledge and sometimes to wrong training methods suggested by someone who claims to be expert but is not. Training must always be done very carefully. Dogs with real problems need teaching by highly skilled and thoughtful methods, or the problems can be made even worse; for all training must be kind, even if it is firm. The wrong kind of teaching can do a great deal of harm but luckily the vast majority of clubs are run by people with a good knowledge of dogs.

One of the most rewarding letters about the book was from Kingston-on-Thames Dog Club asking if I minded them naming a cup for the handler and dog overcoming the most problems – the Chita Cup. It has already been awarded to a dog that started out with a nervous problem and is now happily working with other dogs; a crossbred in this case, mind! I can't think of anything more rewarding. Long after Chita is gone, the cup will remain as her memorial, and the letters telling me who has won it will remind me of the dog I once had; a dog to remember for ever.

One letter is from another of my dog-training friends, Wendy Volhard, who is one of America's top trainers. She has Newfoundlands, which few people over here train for competition. She wrote at Christmas 1980, 'You've obviously worked very hard indeed with Chita and I'm glad you have some real understanding with her.' She adds that Chita is the type of dog she likes but which we see rarely today; (and perhaps, she continues, there is not much place in civilized life for her type, though to the right person it is very rewarding). She met Chita in 1978 at Dorking, when Edith Collins, as she was then, and I went to a seminar given by Wendy and the late Olive Point.

Another reader writes that some of the problems we have are due to the fact that breeders with many dogs in the kennels do not think of their dogs as pet owners do. She points out that the big-name kennels may only bring out dogs for shows, and have no idea of the real personality of the animal as it lives its life in artificial conditions. I thought that a very perceptive letter.

The next letter in the file is from someone who read *Three's A Pack* and commented that she was amazed at how much she agreed with many of my points, and was unaware at the time that she would soon need my help as she later, after reading the book, bought a young German Shepherd bitch that got progressively more scatty from a very early age.

Yet another letter asks for help with yet another bitch. The owner has had thirty-five years of experience with the breed, always having German Shepherd bitches. Her pup was only fourteen weeks old when she wrote. She had just lost her last German Shepherd from epilepsy.

Work in America with guide dog puppies, and research among many litters have shown that the first eight weeks of a puppy's existence have an influence that lasts all its life. The pup that is never handled by humans is dog-conscious and hates humans, or is afraid of them; pups handled by men only may be afraid of women and vice versa; pups mishandled by children or by other dogs or a cat, or handled carelessly or not at all by the breeder, will not be easy to live with as they will have to be tamed. They will have learned that there is too much to fear in life.

Pups need careful handling by kind humans; need to be taught to trust and have fun; need also to be put under very slight stress, such as noise, introduced gradually, as none of us lives in isolation or silence; and well-informed breeders do, on the whole, produce well-balanced puppies. But nobody is perfect; so that there will be mistakes. Those who are honest say, 'I'm sorry; tell me about it so that I can make sure it doesn't happen again.'

My next file contains the reviews. One I appreciated very much came from Richard Askwith, writing in *Gamekeeper and Countryside*; his comments were interesting because he does know about dogs and also he had understood very well what I was writing about, and why I wrote the book. I'm not sure he finds dogs easy to cope with but he will know about training dogs for gunwork. He writes:

> *Three's A Pack* is a very different book to *Two's Company* because while all dogs are difficult and some are completely impossible, Chita seems to have been far worse than average. Mrs Stranger describes her as 'the most dominant bitch I have ever met . . . a baby police dog . . . programmed by its inheritance to attack,' adding that 'Very few

people have met a dog that is so strongly bred to work.'

All too many people would have passed Chita on to someone else as soon as they discovered her latent character, but Mrs Stranger is adamant about the responsibilities of the dog owner; if a dog really is unmanageable you should have it put down, and if you find that unacceptable, you will just have to *make* it manageable. Mrs Stranger took the latter course. To many people, the time and dedication she lavished on an impossible puppy will seem surprising, but in fact *Three's A Pack* shows her to have behaved with the sense of responsibility anyone worthy of owning a dog should possess. Few dog owners need to make the efforts and sacrifices she made for Chita, but every dog owner should be prepared to.

Three's A Pack is an extremely memorable and interesting book, primarily because of the extraordinary and true story it tells. As a study of canine psychology it is probably unique.

You may feel I am bragging to quote that, but in fact authors are far more often demoralized by their reviews than uplifted by them. Nobody who has written as many books as I have is going to be conceited, for the simple reason that one always has some reviews that either are not good, are not there at all, or the reviewer has not quite understood what the author was writing about, especially when it comes to dogs. Some reviewers do not have dogs themselves and may not really be at all interested in the sort of life a dog owner leads. Richard does in fact summarize the points I was trying to bring out, as I feel too many people expect dogs to be easy animals and give up too soon.

One reviewer of *Two's Company* wrote: 'The story of her dogs, told by an author who specializes in writing about animals. YUK!'

So maybe you see why I appreciate Richard's review; and no, I have never met him or even spoken to him on the 'phone!

The other review that particularly pleased me was Sheila Alcock's, writing in *Our Dogs*. I have never met Sheila either but I usually agree with her views. She felt maybe I put too much of myself in the book, but added that without that it would have been hard to understand why I kept Chita. Other types of person would not have done. She commented that this particular puppy is a victim of the demands of nature built into her by successive generations, and is like others of her breeding, which are terrors to live with, as all should be guard dogs or police dogs and require a high degree of skilled training. She picks out unerringly the reason why I did keep Chita. I like her!

Sheila is a breeder, and not a trainer, so she found the details of the various courses I went on fascinating as it was a glimpse into an unknown world. She says 'details of classes, other handlers and teachers, and Chita's response, makes us realize how hard Mrs Stranger had to work.' She then quotes from the books:

Before I had this puppy I would never have dreamed that a young dog could be such a nightmare, and she was a nightmare. But the trouble was that when she wasn't fighting, she was adorable. Never mind, she couldn't get worse, could she? She could and she did as she grew stronger.

[But later on] She comes to me and gazes deep into my eyes. I have found myself quite a dog. She gazes and gazes, leaning on me . . . I don't know what is in her brain . . . but I do know that no other dog I have ever lived with, and I have lost count of the number, has ever trusted me enough to share her bone . . . and her thoughts . . .

Mrs Alcock adds that somewhere between these two extremes lie hours of struggle, frustration, activity in the mud and the cold and the rain, trying to get through to a dog whose whole being is geared to something else, with whom every small success is achievement indeed, even if followed by regression next day.

One reviewer did write that it was unfair to the breed to write this book. But I was writing about *one* particular dog, so that is an unfair comment. I wrote the book *because* I care passionately about the breed. I want to see far better stock, with everyone concerned with quality. Bred well, handled well, cared for well, the German Shepherd is the dog that the police want, not because it is *fierce* but because it is so *trainable*. It is one of the few breeds that can be switched on and off, to show aggression when required, or to play with the baby with absolute safety. Bred ignorantly, the breed can only suffer. Unfortunately, there are a few people who mate to produce a dog resembling an ideal picture, and ignore its mind.

Many dogs that show signs of treachery are in fact ill. Nobody seems to understand that a dog just starting a malignant cancer, not yet detectable to a vet, but very painful, internally, or suffering from a brain tumour, or mental illness, or severe earache, which dogs can suffer too, will become unsafe; *not* because of bad breeding, not because of bad heredity, but because nobody has realized it is in pain. Knocking the site of a growing cancer, or an ear abscess, is agony to the poor animal. It can't speak. It can only react in a dog's way.

Severe arthritis is agony and may make a previously happy dog growly. He may snap instinctively, not meaning to, if you happen to knock those very painful places where it hurts most. Janus has to have his muzzle bandaged if he has sore ears, or he snaps. Yet he is a superbly gentle dog.

My Puma became unreliable but I did *not* put it down to her breed. I was about to have tests done to see if she did have brain trouble, when it became plain that I had to make the hardest decision of all to prevent a disaster. She was put to sleep in March 1981. A post-mortem revealed that she had brain problems. Also she had become blind as a result of that long-ago lead poisoning that caught up with her after all those years. I did have nine years of pleasure from her in spite of that, so it would have been wrong to condemn her when the lead first had effect.

Several dogs I have known have had to die because of becoming unsafe; none were German Shepherds; it happens in all breeds. Every one of these that had a post-mortem proved to have a brain tumour or another major problem. One had a liver cancer that was malignant and pressing on a nerve. The dog can't tell us, and often we can't guess since the only sign of trouble is a change in behaviour. But any change in adult behaviour should be looked at carefully as I suspect that almost every time it is due not to treachery, which dogs don't know about, but to severe pain from internal problems. It may be the sign that the end must come in order to avoid people being harmed; it may in some cases only need veterinary treatment to restore the dog to its previous sweet nature. Ear troubles are frequent, and you can't see a deep ear abscess. It is abominably sore and the dog can't tell you; he can only warn you not to touch that agonizingly painful ear.

We can't enter their world; we have to guess and sometimes we guess wrong.

Chita is now a changed character; no longer the little demon princess, but a dog that I enjoy more and more each day. This book is about her as she is now, and I only mention her as she was to show the difference that training can make. I cannot take all the credit as I had the best help imaginable; I had help from Edith Nicholls, who has changed my life completely; from her husband Bob, who taught Chita manners for the first time, being much stronger than I am. Later, when my little imp was more civilized I had help in preventing her fast reactions from Roy Hunter. In the last chapter I include his summary of Chita. For those in the world that does not include dog training and who will never have heard of him, Roy is very well able to judge a dog's behaviour as he first trained and then instructed the men who have police dogs (from

16

1958 to 1980) for the Metropolitan police.

I first met him when I went on a Working Trials course in Malvern. Chita obviously fascinated him; I got to know him through her; and since then he has come up and given my club a one-day Working Trials course. He and his wife stayed with us for five days during which time he laid tracks for Chita, and helped me a lot and had plenty of chance to observe her, both working and at home.

I will end this chapter with a report that I did not use in *Three's A Pack* as I hoped it might start a book on my reformed character one day; and so it has, and with it is a letter from a friend with whom I stay who had grave doubts about my new puppy four years ago.

Those expecting to read about battles will still find them, but they are only the kind that any owner has with any dog; a desire to go and eat all the time, hopefully; have fun all the time, hopefully; and not to do what the owner wants but what the dog wants, as so many dogs train their owners beautifully to live exactly the way the dog wants them to, and the owner never even realizes it!

The first report is from Ron Tribe, the chairman of Findon Downs Dog Training Club. Ron has bred dogs all his life; his breed is boxers; he is a very knowledgeable man, and also a well-known dog expert.

I visited him when I stayed with Pat O'Shea and Anne Malcolm Bentzen, who became my friends in 1969 when I went down to talk to Findon Dog Club. They have been friends ever since, though we meet rarely; we 'phone and write quite often.

Ron writes of Chita as she was at nine months old. She is now completely changed but it is fascinating to look back and realize how she has altered.

With reference to GSD puppy bitch . . . Chita. I spent one complete evening of about five hours in my own home with Chita and met her again the following day in open country and spent a further three hours with her. The next day I observed her on and off throughout the day at an Open Obedience

Show. I came to the following conclusions:

1. She is a well-made, very well muscled bitch but of small size. I would think it extremely unlikely that she will ever grow to the Standard though she obviously lacks nothing in the way of food and care.

2. Her bone is not as well developed in the leg as I like to see at her age. [This is typical of many modern German Shepherds – J.S.]

3. In character she is somewhat contradictory. Efforts have obviously been made to teach elementary obedience and she will sometimes obey a command given in a normal voice without hesitation. Other times it is necessary to shout the command and repeat it before the desired result is obtained.

4. She shows rather more aggression towards other dogs than she should at this age, allowing for puppy growing-up boisterousness, and she is in consequence quite a handful.

5. Indoors, when one would expect her to settle and rest quietly after a time, she is very restless and whines more or less constantly. Overall my impression is that she is a rather highly strung bitch lacking in the steadiness that should be found in the breed.

6. I should think it undesirable, if not foolish, to breed from her, and I would strongly recommend spaying as soon as veterinary opinions think this suitable.

(signed) R.C. Tribe, Chairman.

I would like to make it plain that Ron Tribe is not a close personal friend. I consulted him as an expert, as an independent authority, who does not breed German Shepherds, though he is an all-round judge. He has a great knowledge of dogs – as dogs, and not as pictures in a book, which is all that a few judges know them as; sometimes they never consider what is in the animal's brain.

Last year I again visited the Malcolm Bentzens and

Pat O'Shea. Anne was away with her Samoyed at a show; but, as before, all three of my dogs came into the house, where Butch greeted them as he always does. He was once a great problem dog, and Pat rescued him. Of all the people I know, she is most in a position to understand what it is like to have to spend time taming a dog, instead of just training him or her.

I asked her to write her opinions of our visit, once Chita had been reformed, as I thought it would be interesting to update her views. She writes:

It's difficult to think of much to say about Chita last year. The Chita that came to visit the first time was more than memorable . . . she was unforgettable. You had to keep her on the lead most of the time in the house and the performance when she had to go in the garden! The second year . . . the year of her transformation, it was the difference in her that was memorable. Last year, well I must confess the most memorable part of the visit as far as the dogs were concerned, was the sight of Puma chasing Chita for a stick and even once taking it away from her. The Chita of the first visit could never have been allowed to play free like that. The point I am trying to make is that then Chita wasn't anything extraordinary, at least not on the surface, a very intense, busy, energetic GSD, not unlike a great many that we have had at the club and that come to our show in June. She was friendly to other dogs, especially Grandad (fourteen-year-old Butch) whom she treated with the greatest respect, she didn't 'do her pieces' (lunge barking to attack them) when people walked their dogs along the footpath on the other side of the road.

Pat ends by saying, because she wrote at one of the down periods of my life, that the things to remember are not the artificial achievements of the various shows, Breed, Obedience and Trials, where luck plays a big part, but the achievements made in giving the dogs a good life and in rehabilitating Chita.

She also adds that the books help many with dogs like mine; and there are many, with dogs in every breed, like any one of the three. I am learning now to live with an old dog; Janus is deaf (really deaf, not just playing at it as dogs can) and sometimes he forgets why he went into the garden so I have to take him out again until he remembers, which can take time; living is a constant learning, or we might as well all be dead. And there is more to learn than any one person could learn in a lifetime.

I was astounded recently by a letter read on the 5 p.m. programme by someone who could only be very young and green, commenting on the fact that senior citizens were bemoaning the loss of some of their education programmes. This young lady added that if you haven't learned enough by sixty then heaven help you, as you should by then know everything!

I wondered if she had given up learning; there are thousands of dogs I have never watched; dozens of breeds I have never met; hundreds of hours of work that could be done to add to my knowledge, and even then I will just have lifted the curtain on all the lore that any one person can gain in a lifetime of much more than threescore years and ten. (I'm nowhere near there yet!)

The next dog I have will teach me new lessons; Chita has taught me so much; she has increased my confidence, she has made me take up trouble-shooting with dogs, which is something I had never contemplated; she has made me think deeply and she had made me far more considerate of others with problems caused not by their own faults, but because they bought a dog that nobody could have taken on. She has helped me into a new occupation as Edith Nicholls and I are now partners, and we are seething with plans to help pet dog owners. Most of those dogs like Chita are put down and it may not be necessary; those that survive need careful management all their lives.

On one memorable occasion Chita towed Roy Hunter back to me; and he is a strong tough ex-police-dog handler; I watched him sail along at a speed that was almost out of control, my dog pulling out in front of him, Roy trying to get her back and having to fight her strength! Later I tried her on one of his well made and very strong tracking harnesses, of webbing, far more reasonable in price than the very expensive leather ones. Chita caught the scent of the track and leaped out on the end of her line, driving fast, and pulled the D-ring straight.

Roy looked at me as I handed him a harness with a straight D-ring and said, 'I don't believe it.' But it happened; he saw it happen; she is immensely strong and all her life Chita will need to go only to those who can handle dogs; those who can take real care of her, and understand her needs. I only know of three people I would trust her to if I were unable to look after her, which would only happen if I had to go into hospital for a long spell.

This is her story as she is now, and all I can say is, 'Boy, she's quite a dog!'

Chapter Two

If I were a fairy godmother there are only two virtues I would wish on any child. Courage and a sense of humour.

A sense of humour should include the ability to laugh at oneself on occasion; it doesn't do to take life too seriously. A lot of it is funny and none of us are all that important to anyone but ourselves.

I find sometimes I am misunderstood because I do laugh at myself and I do laugh at my dogs. I lived most of my early life in Kent, surrounded by people who were often Cockney in their sense of humour; and Cockneys don't have either a sense of self-importance or an awe of people who think they are important! Pomposity brings out the worst in us.

It can get one into trouble at times.

That terrible Cockney imp gets hold of me, so that with a poker face, I can say something that is taken quite the wrong way by someone who has never learned that unless you regard a lot of life as a joke, life itself becomes impossible.

'I don't know how you could stand it. I would have *died*,' someone assures me solemnly, at a Ladies Luncheon, where everyone is wearing the sort of hat that mesmerizes me and takes my mind off what I was going to say. I have just described in what I hoped was hilarious detail how I staggered, in my bathing costume, along a country lane, hanging on to a onetime pet lamb who is now a nine-year-old, vast, lame, and very smelly ewe.

Her name was Bessie and she was about to be dipped.

The farmer's brother had forgotten they were going to dip the sheep and had gone off for the day taking all the farm dogs with him, which was remarkably helpful all round.

'You can help,' the farmer assured us, roping in myself and the three children. We were used to sheep and knew what to do but we aren't as fast as dogs.

Bessie had gone walkabout, no doubt having already smelled the sheepdip.

It was, luckily, a really glorious summer day, and we were in Pembrokeshire. The sea was blue: the cliffs bright with sea thrift in pink tussocks, the waves broke in soft murmurs on the sands; and we were on the fields above the beach.

The farmhouse baked in the sun and the yard was full of sheep all yelling that they didn't want to be dipped, thank you very much. The lambs, who hadn't met this before and weren't part of the exercise anyway, yelled for their mothers, and broke away to join them. One pair of fine well-grown ram lambs, sure mother was being killed, came to her rescue. One stood on her head and one stood on her rump and she submerged, bleating and choking, and we had a hair-raising five minutes. Rams determined not to move seem to have a remarkable number of parts than can damage humans who don't have hooves.

Meanwhile Bessie had gone up the lane.

'*You* get her back,' the farmer said.

It seemed so simple till I reached her; as by then she had managed to get herself into the ditch and being old and cross and unco-operative, had no desire to get out. I hauled her by her woolly coat which she didn't like; I had horrible visions of the wool coming out in tufts, but it didn't, and finally I did manage to pull her on to the road, where all I got was a baleful look and a kick as she yanked herself free and set off in the wrong direction. How I wished I had the dog. Dogs do it so easily once trained.

Meanwhile the whole of the farm seemed to be watching, laughing and clapping.

My own children were convulsed.

So I suspect was Bessie.

We set off again, me coming a bad second. I wasn't really dressed for chasing an old ewe down the road and it amused the passing motorists.

In through a cottage gate, down the path and into the hall.

I prayed for continence.

I managed to get my hands interwined in her wool and coax her out, before she damaged anything. Nobody seemed to be about. The cottage was immaculate, everywhere polished till it shone; newly arranged flowers stood on a table in the little hall. I negotiated them, praying hard.

I dragged Bessie out of the gate and closed it and I lugged her, protesting, every inch of the long road back to the farm. The gate was opened and expert hands took her off me, sent her up the plank and into the dip and she revenged herself by shaking all the surplus dip from her heavy fleece all over me.

Every time I met the farmer on that holiday he went off into peals of laughter.

'I'm sorry,' he'd say, wiping his eyes. 'But you did look so funny with that old ewe of mine; she's a one, is Bessie.'

I hadn't nearly died of shame as my hearer at the luncheon would have done. (She wouldn't have been there!) I found it funny too, and we stood there, in the yard, laughing together; I knew I must have been one of the most amusing sights that day; and Bessie, who had never learned to respect people, knew it too. She had been brought up on the bottle and had all a pet lamb's annoying habits, of preferring human food to her own, human company to that of sheep, coupled with a strong will and a desire to get her own way; humans had to watch out when they came into her life.

She reminded me of another occasion long before when my mother and father-in-law had come to stay and we had gone out, while the children were at school, for a picnic on the Derbyshire moors. We discovered, very rapidly, that the only place safe from marauding sheep was the car. The sheep were used to picnickers, and if you didn't give them food, they ganged up and took it. If you were unco-operative they butted and bit.

While we were eating, a number of police cars went by.

With some misgivings, we watched them. Were they looking for an escaped convict, or an escaped lunatic? Or was something even more sinister going on?

Then we spotted the L plates. They were having driving instruction.

In due course they parked, not very far from us, and a remarkable number of policemen got out of the cars, stretched their legs, walked around, and then took out packs of sandwiches. We watched with interest as the sheep rioted.

The policemen were not prepared to deal with rioting sheep. They took shelter as we had in the cars, grinning at us, obviously now aware as to why these fools sat inside on a nice day, and refused to come out while they were eating.

One sergeant was determined he would eat in the fresh air.

He ended up sitting on top of a high wall, cross-legged, looking extremely uncomfortable, while the sheep put their fore-hooves on the stones and seemed to be trying to knock the wall down. Everyone was helpless with laughter.

But this story, when told to my lunchtime ladies, didn't even raise a smile.

As a result I began to keep my experiences with dogs, which could be much worse, rather dark. The dogs and I enjoyed a joke together but everyone else seemed determined to take every event seriously. Some of course, I do take seriously, but most of living is so absurd that it isn't worth getting in a state over. Even the benefits of civilization can produce ridiculous effects.

I picked up the ringing 'phone this week, and a voice, with a strong accent, after a remarkable number of paypips said 'Are you expecting visitors from Ireland who haven't come?'

'No.'

'Then you're the wrong person,' he said, and rang off, leaving me somewhat surprised and feeling disbelief. He could only be Irish – I love most of them but they do have the strangest logic!

So I decided to go shopping and go to my favourite bookshop and find something lighthearted to read, as I am tired of spies and holocausts and nuclear disasters and deep political treatises, and books that seem to get nastier and nastier about rats and plagues and death and doom and destruction. I can live that through the TV news; I want to be cheered and entertained, and briefly taken out of a world that gets increasingly unnerving.

So off I went, my dogs in the back of the car.

I parked in Beaumaris which is a Victorian seaside town; on the green, near the sea, having just paid 30p. I had vaguely noticed a few ponies tethered on the green. I pulled on the handbrake and killed the engine. The dogs barked.

I turned round.

I was looking, with some astonishment, at the three animals in front of me, only a hundred yards away, tethered like goats.

A camel, a llama, and a zebra.

The camel looked extremely odd, as one hump drooped over its side, giving it a slightly dismal appearance.

I turned my head and was relieved to see a large trailer with somebody's circus advertised on it. For one moment, I really thought I was seeing things.

I walked past them (all as quiet as goats too) across the green to the shops. I looked at the ground, as it was necessary to take great care where you trod, and thought of the number of letters there are each year about dogs fouling such places. The writers should just have seen this!

I shopped, and came back with books, apples and strawberries, crossing the green, feeling that at times life itself was as irrational as this experience and that we are all victims of a new society where anything might happen.

Technology doesn't help make life any more believable.

I have just, after two years, I think and hope, managed to stop the computer that has been dunning me faithfully every month for a bill that I paid by return of post on receiving the goods I had ordered.

When I complained about an income tax demand threatening to sue me I was told that that department is on a different floor to the one that takes in the cheques and that was why I had been told I was to be sued for tax I had paid over a month before.

It all adds to the fun, I suppose.

Dogs definitely add to it, but if you have a Golden Retriever dog, you need more appreciation of fun than most people, I suspect. Retrievers have a sense of humour all their own; they don't respect people; and many seem to set out in life determined to make sure that as many odd events centre round them as they can manage.

Not that I would ever be without a retriever; maybe you get used to being made a fool of!

Janus could always make a fool of me beautifully. He loved retrieving. After all, he *is* a retriever, still, even at almost eleven, and deaf and very awkward in his old age.

This, however, was not his old age. He was about four and supposedly in his heyday. We were competing in a show.

It was hot.

Very hot.

Only a fool, said Janus's attitude, would expect any dog to work on a day like this. There is a lake over there.

'And you are staying here,' I told him. All this being done by our eyes. He looked at the lake again and I said NO under my breath and added 'don't you dare' inside my head.

I knew my dog only too well.

'Throw your bell,' said the steward, unaware of the silent argument. Other dogs had already been in the lake. It was very tempting.

I threw the dumbbell and Janus watched it go. It fell conveniently close to a large clump of damp grass; a very large clump. The wood was painted white and it showed up beautifully.

Janus sauntered out.

It was to be one of his slow motion days. He could, if he chose, do things at a slower pace than I believed possible for any dog; except of course when we were asked to *do* slow pace, when he pricked up his ears and heard imaginary martial music and had to be restrained from marching out at a cracking speed.

Janus arrived at the dumbbell and eyed it.

If he went round the back, he could lie down in the long grass, which was blissfully cool and moist, and put his head on his dumbbell and close his eyes and have a small snooze. So he did.

The steward made a noise that was a cross between a snort and snuffle.

I stared in disbelief and the judge rolled his eyes heavenwards in the sort of look that says 'We've got a right one here.'

'Janus!' I needed to shout. I knew his mood only too well.

He stood up, looked at me, picked up the dumbbell, and with a look of infinite suffering, took it to the judge, instead of bringing it to me.

After years of Janus, I knew that I never ever could have another dog like him. They just didn't happen.

Puma proved me wrong.

Puma, not a Golden Retriever, but a very impressive and apparently dignified German Shepherd bitch, had, unnervingly, a different sense of humour all her own. It was nothing like Janus's. Now Puma is dead I miss sharing her jokes.

In her heyday Puma also was no respecter of persons and could make this very clear indeed.

There I was with Puma, in the Obedience ring. She was a bitch shown in Breed, and I didn't train her for Obedience, but she worked it and she did quite well. I never forced her as I didn't want her Breed showing

28

spoiled; I wasn't as experienced then. I wouldn't hesitate to train a dog for both if I wanted, now.

We had a very small judge wearing a very large picture hat.

I knew we were in for trouble before we began as Puma had her eyes on that hat and she couldn't take them off it. She was dancing with amusement, prancing along, full of fun and naughtiness, her eyes glittering with happiness and obvious hilarity.

'Have you seen that *hat*?' her eyes said.

I told her to sit, trying to keep my face quite straight and hoping *my* eyes didn't betray us.

The judge was behind us.

Puma turned her head and completely missed my command to start off.

Halfway round, the judge still behind us, marching along looking for faults, Puma turned her head again. She wasn't doing her usual fairly sedate walk, but a dancing trot, scarcely able to contain herself.

Every time she sat by my side on my command she sneaked another look behind and then looked up at me.

I couldn't manage to keep my own face quite under control, as the judge was smaller than I was and all I could see was the hat. All Puma could see was from below and I began to wonder what she could see and what she really thought and that was the end of my concentration. Her eyes gleamed with what could only be laughter.

We disgraced ourselves completely and have never had such a bad score.

'Have you *trained* that bitch?' the judge asked in such a withering tone that I nearly collapsed into laughter and disgraced us even more.

'Yes,' I said, with considerable difficulty, hoping my eyes weren't betraying me as Puma's did her.

'Well, I don't think much of your training.'

It was more than I could bear; I couldn't even thank her for the round. My friends watched as I doubled up with laughter, leaning against my car and Puma danced round me, behaving in a totally uncharacteristic fashion as she rarely allowed herself to be undignified in public.

I never dared work her under a judge in any kind of hat again.

When I got a third dog, I hoped that this one would not have a sense of humour. It can be very difficult to cope with in public.

Chita showed little sign of it at first. I ended *Three's A Pack* when she was two years old and I was still battling with a determined little madam who thought she had been born to boss every dog and every human and every other creature she met.

Two years later I seem to have another dog with a sense of humour all her own. It has developed with experience and maturity.

Though perhaps it stems from me; I can only share my jokes as a rule with people who were brought up where I was brought up; humour is very regional. My father's sense of humour was unique!

There was I with Chita at yet another Obedience show, a few weeks ago. In the 'summer' of 1981.

Everyone was remarkably wet; we signed on in a cattle truck, walking through acres of mud to get to it; everything was rather primitive, the fields were in the middle of nowhere and the cars were on the lane by the fields, and miles from where we wanted to be, so nobody could shelter.

In one field the pony club was struggling against the weather, without sympathy, as a wet dog is easier to dry than a soaked pony and soaked tack. The jumping also looked hazardous. We only had to walk round the fields, and round the ring where we were to perform.

Janus is retired, an old man, allowed to rest on his laurels. He had a walk long enough to tire him out, sniffing at the new smells, very interested in something through the wire, out of his reach, of course, and so much more interesting than what was in reach.

I persuaded him he didn't really want to climb through the barbed wire and that he would be much more comfortable dried off with a towel and lying in the car. Chita meanwhile was yelling that nobody loved her, she was all alone and when was I coming?

I told her to be quiet, and she was, for nearly half a second.

At four, she is still full of drama.. A real prima donna type.

Me, look at me, all the time.

I took her out and she discovered that her friends the King Charlies were in the next car, and had a sniff through the windows. I discouraged her, as I didn't think the King Charlies' owners would be pleased to find mud all over their car.

We ducked under the wire, navigated the mud, negotiated the edge of the pony club ring, avoided several hooves and a trotting pony, and came to our own field, where I discovered I was unpopular. I got the times wrong and we had all missed the classes we entered for, because the Obedience started at 11.00 a.m.; unlike the Breed which started at 1.00 p.m. I couldn't find the times for the Obedience and thought it all began at 1.00 p.m.

Nobody was very cross; we had to go in classes higher than those we work normally, which meant Chita was about to do scent for the first time in her life; as well as a variety of other things I haven't yet taught her. The result was predictable. She did a Working Trials search beautifully!

The ring was not only muddy but wet.

Puddles; reminding me of Basingstoke three years ago when I was offered a choice as I went in to work. A choice? 'Yes,' said the judge, a man after my own heart, with a poker face and a sense of humour. 'Do you want to do backstroke or crawl?'

It was that sort of day again.

'DOWN,' shouts the steward.

'In a puddle, no thank you,' said Chita with her very expressive little body, marching forward four paces, arranging her skirts very carefully and gingerly sitting, her tail slightly above the ground. I wondered what the judge made of that and we went on. Chita negotiated another puddle; obviously she thought she needed the canine equivalent of Sir Walter Raleigh and his cloak. As it was she stepped as daintily as a cat. (She is extremely dainty.)

'DOWN,' shouted the steward.

Chita looked at me. 'That puddle again,' as we were round the ring again. We went through the same performance, me slightly distracted by her determination not to drop in water. Other dogs just did it and got wet.

It was time for her recall and her retrieve. The recall could have been worse; a bit worse. She hadn't done it that way before. 'That's big girls' way, and I'm a little girl still,' her eyes said indignantly after she had worked out that yes, I was calling her to my heel from behind, instead of to sit in front of me, facing me, as we normally do.

'Clever girl.'

'Well, of course,' she said, tossing her head.

Dogs may not talk and may not use our language and may not be human, but humans can be quite like dogs at times!

Now for the retrieve. She loves that.

Bob, who was judging us, was in the centre of the ring, looking extremely odd in a borrowed mackintosh resembling a tent, and wearing a hat that hid his face; you could just see his mouth and eyes if you peered beneath the rim. It added to the absurdity of the day. Niagara Falls appeared to have been transferred to the sky above us.

Chita watched her dumbbell thrown and careered out, full of the joy of living.

She does everything with flair, everything with verve, everything with determination and this was no exception, except she got sidetracked.

She stopped with the air of a pantomime giant, her head up, sniffing.

'Fee fi fo fum, there's something in the wind, I know that smell, and where's it from and what am I going to find?'

She sniffed again, and then turned and pointed her nose at Bob.

She knows Bob. He is part of her life. She loves Bob. 'Bob. It's Bob. It's my friend Bob.' She arrived and dug her nose into his clothing, just to check, and then did a wild leap to lick his ear, which is her form of greeting; it puts a lot of people off and I have to watch her and stop it. Help, being attacked by a savage beast.

In fact they are being adored, prior to being washed all over their faces and ears.

Bob stood completely still, being a judge, and said 'What on earth do you think you are doing?' and Chita appeared to say 'Whoops, sorry,' and came to sit in front of me and look up.

'Aren't I *good*?' Her eyes pleaded for praise. She now loves praise and works for it and not for titbits.

'Dumbbell, you horrible animal.'

'Oh, yes,' she said, her eyes gleaming with laughter, reminding me of Puma, which I wished she hadn't done as Puma was too newly dead. Off she trotted, picked it up with a tremendous air of concentration, never-did-anything-wrong air, and brought it in and sat.

Bob's poker face collapsed and I 'finished' her in a gale of laughter.

'Honestly, Chita!'

I really didn't think it could happen three times; not three dogs like that in one person's lifetime.

She couldn't do much worse, could she?

She could. A week later we had visitors and one of our visitors was going to the Colwyn Bay Show with me; and has a large, very happy German Shepherd dog. He is beautiful and Chita had to fall in love.

Being a dramatic bitch she did it wholeheartedly, following him everywhere and yearning. 'Isn't he gorgeous?' Her eyes adored him and she turned to look at me. 'Isn't he handsome? Have you ever seen anything like him?' Her body was eloquent. I remembered our daughter's teenage passions, and hoped that Chita wasn't going to put me through the same sort of thing as it could distract from her show results as badly as Janus's frequent bitch passions detracted from his. 'Can't work. There's a bitch . . . oh, she's lovely.'

We went to the show together. It was in Eirias Park in Colwyn Bay which is a really lovely venue; short grass, plenty of room and shade under the trees for parking cars. It was hot and sunny for the first time that year and everyone was relaxed. It was all that a show ought to be. The organization was excellent and there were people there I hadn't seen for ages as I hadn't travelled so far this year. Everything was wonderful except that for some reason Janus was working sixth and I had not put him in for competition. I must have left out the necessary magic initials NFC (not for competition) on my form, or else put him in a class from force of habit, as I have been doing it for him now for nine years.

Worse, Chita was now even more bemused by love. Or its doggy equivalent. Whatever the feeling, the end result is the same; all the distraction you get in the human race when they become besotted!

I told the judge my dog was old and not really there to work but as we had come up in the draw to work in the first ten we would try. She was charming, and after watching his efforts she realized I hadn't intended to enter him and wasn't just making things up to excuse him. He managed beautifully on the lead, but off lead, unable to hear a word I said, and with me not supposed to touch him, we came to grief. He pottered happily from smell to smell, gazing round him with his old assurance that everyone adored him, his tail wagging happily, an old dog on a fine day doing just what he liked.

I put him in a sit for the recall and called him to me across the ring. He couldn't hear a sound so he knew he was meant to stay where he was, and did so with the obvious conviction that he was doing wonderfully well. I had to go to him, and as everyone laughed he saw their faces and knew that was what he should have done and wagging happily watched me get his dumbbell from the table. He adores retrieving and he knew that exercise backwards and did it very well.

But he forgot he should come in fast and had a little game on the way back and if you can't when you are old, when can you? The judge laughed too and his marks remain a secret; we didn't bother with the *stays*.

He came out of the ring and was petted by my friends from our dog club, and came back to the car, as pleased as if he were carrying a red rosette. He had done enough for the day and settled happily to sleep in the shade under the trees.

It was time to work my lovelorn little bitch.

Usually these days she works well and comes in the first ten, out of about fifty or sixty, but that day she had her mind on other things. Her beloved had an owner who was exceptionally busy, trotting all over the place, appearing just when I least expected it in a place I hadn't expected her, and Chita's head reminded me of the watchers at Wimbledon. 'There he is, no, look, he's over there, oh, there he is in that ring, no he's gone to the coffee table; now he's coming towards us, oh, he's gone again.' If a dog could talk with its body then Chita did, as she veered from eager expectation to drooping dismay as he went out of sight again.

It was too funny to bother with the fact that her marks were terrible. The judge was understanding, and my club members knew how Chita could work on her good days, so it didn't worry me much. We didn't usually go to shows with that particular dog and I would take care not to again, or I would be wasting my money, as being Chita she wouldn't forget him. I only hope we don't meet at Trials as that could also affect her, especially if they ended up in the stay line together.

We did most of the beginner round and came to the retrieve. She ran out for the dumbbell. 'Oh, there he is again, isn't he lovely? Oh, he's gone again.' A few more commands and she did remember she had gone out for her dumbbell and not to admire her distant beloved. She brought it in. I took her out of the ring and then as I joined my club members again, we dissolved in laughter as off went her loved one at a fast gallop across the field and she followed. So, perforce did I, lead outstretched, me doing a Chita curse as that was something she hadn't done for about a year and she is extremely strong. She had the bit between her teeth, if there is a dog equivalent of that, and was well away.

We reached our destination.

She took one sniff and her tail dropped.

'It isn't *him*.'

It was his double. His owner looked slightly amazed at the speed with which we arrived and the attitude with which we left. I couldn't see Chita's passion or his owner; I had told her I wasn't working the novice round but was going to scratch. I went to find the judge.

I knew the novice judge from our Cheshire days and he persuaded me to take Chita in just for experience; both for her and me. It wouldn't do any harm after all. I thought she was feeling sick, as whenever she lay down she took a quick snack of grass, and had to be stopped. It is another of her more annoying habits, and very difficult to break as she's so fast.

She had produced one or two experimental heaves, and I didn't want her to be sick in the ring.

'She seems all right at the moment,' the judge said quite rightly. 'If she is sick you can run. Do work her. I haven't seen her before anyway. And you are last before the stays.' He's a super judge, with the right attitude, so I did work Chita; she didn't do badly but she didn't do anything like her normal round and as I said we weren't going to work, her passion turned up again and distracted her completely all down one side of the ring, as his owner stood chatting with her back to us! Someone else watching us was as amused as I was; Chita showed her feelings in her expression and her attitude and was extremely funny.

One problem I often find is that those who take shows very seriously interpret my comments on her in the way they would have felt if it had happened to them. Consequently I can never make some people understand that they aren't feeling as I do but as they would have felt if their own dog had behaved as mine did! I'm entertained and having fun.

But often competitors can be like the lady who would have died if Bessie the sheep had played her up as she did me. Or those who were appalled at another luncheon when I had to talk (it is very difficult to talk to people who live totally different lives from yourself). I was telling them how, some years before, I had spent a holiday in a nature reserve in Ireland. My host had built a hide in a tree.

The tree was on a hummock over a badger sett and I went there, climbing up by ladder, at about 10.00 p.m. just before dark. I wanted to see the badgers. I didn't, but I heard a phenomenal badger fight, somewhere underneath my tree, about midnight. At 1.00 a.m. I was still there; cramped and cold and it was windy and spooky, though the house was within sight, but not within shouting distance.

Something brushed against the tree. It proved to be Billy bullock. I was quite sorry when he left. My host finally did remember me and arrived full of apologies with the ladder to get me out of the tree and into the warm. He said he hadn't gone to bed and forgotten me, but we teased him all week about it.

Nobody at the luncheon thought it in the least funny. I don't think anyone could even visualize wanting to spend part of the night in a tree looking for badgers either!

Even when I went to America the funniest part of the visit centred round dogs and cats and a skunk; not to mention pheasants as big as turkeys. The cocktail party I went to was enlivened by an Abyssinian kitten and a Burmese cat with a fondness for pâté and olives. We spent a good deal of the evening fielding cats from the table.

It was extremely amusing, but people who prefer pâté and olives to eat don't appreciate the joke!

Eventually I gave up trying to explain I wasn't upset by Janus's antics; who in their senses could expect an eleven-year-old to work in competition? Some can;

but he is an old man now and beyond it.

I gave up explaining that I wasn't unduly worried by Chita's performance; I hope my novice judge realized that; he did try to console me, but I had knowledge of other recent shows where she had come fifth, fourth and third and put up an excellent showing; nobody can produce the perfect result all the time and even champions have their off days. She is by no means at Crufts standard, but her efforts now reward *me*.

What I was concerned with was her stay performance as that is one of our major problems and one that could prevent her ever qualifying as I want; and the difficulty isn't now due to her; it's due to other people's dogs fighting beside her when she was in a stay position. Unnerving for any dog, but most unnerving of all for a dog that used to be a fear fighter, going for other dogs to prevent them going for her first.

Now she backs off when she is attacked and relies on me to sort matters out, which is infinitely preferable as long as the other dog has an owner with it. Those without owners need locking up; they cause untold harm to dogs whose owners care about them. They are more of a menace to dog owners than to those who don't have dogs, as a rule.

A stray local dog at a show is an absolute pest. Luckily the vast majority of trained dogs have been taught to ignore them.

We left the ring that day and went to the stay ring. Chita wasn't happy; she was most unhappy. She did her sitstay, without any problem; and this was in Obedience where she had been so steady she had been placed three times. But that fight next to her had happened since the last trials; we were practising among twenty other dogs, and the dog attacked was lying next to her; and being a terrier type he fought back. Chita stayed, rigid, terrified while the din was going on all round her.

This was to be the first stay at a show since.

I knew she wasn't happy on sitstays but she did stay.

Two people from my club who knew my problem suggested I put her between their two very steady King Charles spaniels, as she knew them; but it was plain before I left her that she would disturb every other dog; she cried and she crawled, she was in a blind panic and then she began to heave.

I had to take her out and presently she was sick; there was no way I could make her stay alone until I had built up her confidence again and that meant that we had to go right back to the beginning.

She had been in five Trials stakes by then and she had had a major stay problem at first. There is a letter from one of my judges in the last chapter of this book. He knew what I had to contend with; she cannot bear me going out of her sight when she is in a strange place. She is unhappy with people she doesn't know and with dogs she has never met before and some of them are unsteady too and disturb her.

Yet only a few weeks before we had almost qualified and she had done her sitstay and nearly all her downstay, when again the unforeseen happened. She was sick after eight minutes with me out of sight. I had thought we had cracked that problem.

Now it is all to do again.

Perhaps that will be our story right through; I hope in years to come we will have got over her unhappiness when I vanish from her view at Trials or a show; she isn't by any means unique in not staying.

As ever, we go back to training. If we don't make it, it won't be the end of the world. There is so much else to do; and I won't make winning prizes with my dogs the be-all and end-all of my existence.

Shows and Trials are a hobby; my dogs are a hobby. They are an important part of my life but not the only part. When it became plain that Puma was going to be a liability to humans and might end up damaging one badly, Puma, I knew, had come to the end of her allotted time in this world.

I could have locked her in a kennel; but she loved me too much for me to condemn her to solitary confinement. To me, that was crueller by far than death.

She didn't suffer at the end; she died peacefully in my arms, freed, we now know, from the pain that had become constant in her life; those of us who are left suffer, but my dogs won't live on merely because I am afraid of suffering from their deaths; they can't live for ever, and to me it is kinder by far to say 'now', with the vet's full approval, than to wait until the dog is in agony, or until pain drives it to attack and injure a human. It no longer knows what it is doing.

Dogs have a place in our lives, but it must be in proportion and the day I change my dog for an easy one because I didn't win first prize is the day I know that I no longer have a proper sense of values and my priorities are wrong. And I can no longer train a dog to be my companion.

I value Puma's prizes and her championship certificate; it is a once in a lifetime thing and I was delighted when she won it; but my memories of her are not of shows, but of the bitch by my side who gave me her devotion and who meant much more to me than a few red ribbons.

At every show in a class of sixty there are fifty-nine who didn't win. So, to those who are among the fifty-nine, read what Roy Hunter said and take heart and courage and hold your heads high, because you are learning the right way what life is really about.

Edith Nicholls said at the end of her write-up in *Three's A Pack*, 'Success only comes before toil in dictionaries.'

This account is of our toil; and there is still a long way to go.

I keep a book of cut out photographs that have interested me; of poems by other people and little pieces that make me feel better if I am down. One that is pasted in, by an unknown author, came from the *German Shepherd Weekly* in 1978 and the last two lines I have typed and put where I can read them daily.

Stick to the fight; when you're hardest hit,
It's when things seem worst that you must not quit.

It's followed by a letter from someone who wrote to me the night that he found his little cat dead on the road. He is an old man; and he sat with his other cat on his knee, reading *Khazan*. It took his mind off his sorrow and he ended his letter by thanking me for writing a book that had helped him that night over a very bad patch, even 'though it was a cat that most people wouldn't have given a second look.' It had been his cat. He had cared about it. And I feel the hours of writing had been worth every minute, to help someone like that.

That is what living is about.

The next letter is from someone who didn't even give his address as he felt I should not have to answer him; he wanted to thank me for being allowed to see a little of my world through my eyes as he shared many of my thoughts about animals, and had enjoyed the book (which was about my long dead Siamese, Kym, who was a feline Chita) very much indeed.

Reading the letters on *Kym* and on the two dog books, I know there are many people who, like Sheila Alcock, want to know what happened next; and hopefully, one day, we will have gone on and persisted and can write the book that Roy wants to see, and that Edith wants to see; titled 'Success with Chita', or perhaps 'High Scores'. We have already had a few of those.

Meanwhile we hope; and for those who are on the same track as I am, with dogs that look as if they will never win, here perhaps you might find pointers to your needs. This is the story of a reformed imp who teaches me all the time, and who, I suspect, will never stop teaching me, as she is very much a dog with a mind of her own.

Chapter Three

Most people, I find, tend to keep their dogs' doings rather dark, not wanting to confess to the more awful experiences, but they do happen to all of us. Experience makes little odds. Recently someone came to judge our club progress night. She is one of the greatest experts I know in the world of dogs, and she brought her husband's dog with her. On the way he happened to encounter a bitch near to season.

His behaviour that evening was far from ideal.

Being a dog, we had to put up with it and tell him off when his ideas became too outrageous. As he was tied up beside Chita, who happens to be a bitch, even if a spayed bitch, and to have her own ideas on what to do about flirting (she does so, quite outrageously) it was an interesting evening to say the least.

On another occasion I was on a course given by someone who is probably one of the most experienced of all competitors in the Obedience world. Unfortunately his competition dog is at stud and that day a bitch had come into the kennels to be mated. No matter what he tried to do with his dog, every exercise ended in the same way. At the gate to the kennels, asking plainly to be allowed to go and get on with his real work, instead of wasting time with this silly nonsense.

Dogs are dogs. And nothing we can do will change them in that respect. We can overcome instincts by hard work; we can make them biddable and obedient but with a young dog, an untrained dog, or a stud dog with a bitch waiting for him, even the most experienced trainer can find that nothing will influence the dog.

We did check the two flirts; and they did behave themselves, but they kept forgetting and having to be reminded. The stud dog finally was allowed to go off to the kennels. His bitch wasn't ready for him, so he had to be put alone to wait as patiently as he could. There was no way in which his mind would come off the bitch and on to practising for a competition.

Janus used to be very bitch conscious and if we were at a Breed show, as many of the Obedience shows have German Shepherd breed rings as well, I often had no chance at all. He would walk round with his nose in the air looking like the Bisto Kid; 'Cor, I can smell *bitch*. Isn't it *lovely*?' Any resemblance to actually doing as he should have done was pure coincidence. A lot of people suffer from the same thing with dogs when bitches are around, but they don't always realize what has made the poor dog so distracted.

People who have had only bitches and not dogs rarely realize what problems they can pose for the dog owner. Dogs will howl all night if a nearby bitch is in season; they will go gadabout on their own, hopefully travelling miles if there is the scent of a bitch on the wind, and it can travel over surprisingly large distances. They become totally oblivious to normal needs and will even starve themselves. One dog I knew well used to go into a decline when the family bitch was in season.

She was penned, and he spent the three weeks lying with his nose as close to the pen as he could get, his muzzle through the wire, and ate nothing at all until it was over. He looked dreadful at the end of three weeks, but there was nothing anyone could do about it.

One neighbour of ours, when her bitch was in season, was used to seeing the nose of the town scruff come through the letter-box and be trapped as the flap had a powerful spring. He would lie there till released and then ten minutes later trap himself again!

I grew used to having Janus behave as if nothing existed but the scent of bitch on the wind. When we were at shows without Breed classes he did well. A lot of people used to moan about their dogs and I don't think some of them ever realized that it genuinely was bitch scent and not cussedness that made the dogs behave so badly. You could cure it by borrowing in-season bitches non-stop and making the dog work by force, but it never seemed to me worth the effort! Apart from anything else few of my friends would have been willing to lend me their bitches just to make sure my dog could do a number of rather formal exercises in spite of the scent of bitch on the air.

I wrote a doggerel rhyme once about it, which appeared in a couple of magazines. I can't find the printed version and may not be able to remember it all, but it did amuse quite a few people, and went something like this:

A Dog's Prayer to his Master

I'm out on the field, and I haven't a care.
There's the glorious scent of a bitch on the air.
I'm running in circles and sniffing the ground,
For news of my rivals. Who *has* been around?
Hang on a mo! I'll just add my share.

That's funny. Where's master? Oh, he's over there.
He's standing, he's glaring, his lips are clenched tight,
And so are his fists. He looks ready to fight.
There's the judge . . . and the steward . . . O Sirius! O No!
I forgot all about it. We're in the ring, at a show.

O master, dear master, don't fume and don't fret.
I'll do all that you ask me, and win that rosette.
I'll haste to obey you, and do it with pride.
I'll not make mistakes and I'll stay by your side.
But master, dear master, I've got a good reason.
How the hell can I work with that bitch there in season?

It really is hard sometimes!
Bitches are far easier to manage in the same circumstances. They don't pose half the problems you can get with a dog. They can still show all the signs of being in love!

We have just had our two-year-old granddaughter

44

staying with us; the problems that come from human babies and puppies are very similar. Morag is an explorer by nature, which might stand her in good stead when she is grown up but certainly doesn't while she is a toddler and doesn't know what is safe to do and what is not. Open the garden gate and vanish down the road and we may well have a dead baby on our hands, run over by a car. Open the door to the garden and she might end in the river.

Children need constant vigilance at this stage. Later when she understands 'no', it will be easier. 'No' must be taught to babies and to puppies.

Small children also manage to hurt dogs without meaning to. Morag was curious and wanted to explore mouths and eyes; luckily both our dogs put up with an amazing amount from the babies, even Janus, who is not really very fond of either children or puppies. He would stand so much and then go to his bed, asking to be left in peace. Chita allowed fingers to explore her ears and eyes, and even her nose, and all she did was to lick the children. She was more patient than I expected.

Her early problems with people were due to misunderstanding as she thought she was being stolen if anyone took her off me. She still does, but she now screams to come to me and pulls hard on her lead, refusing to go with anybody else. She is my dog and I belong to her. She can be remarkably noisy if she thinks people don't understand what she is trying to tell them.

There is nothing quite like the chorus Chita can make with Chia, our blue point Siamese when both are hungry. Chia also has a mind of her own and a voracious appetite, which has to be curbed as if she is overfed she has a non-stop sick which is extremely trying, so we ration her. She would eat till she is sick and not only does she expect to be fed when the dogs are fed, when we are fed and in between as well, but if anyone goes into the kitchen Chia is convinced we have gone there to feed her; and Janus is convinced we have gone there to cut him a slice of brown bread, as he is addicted to it, beyond the normal desire of a dog for food. If Chia yells, Chita often helps her. 'We want *food*.' Proper little Oliver Twists. 'More, more, more!' Many animals are greedy.

If we lose Janus in the evening we find him sitting bolt upright, ears cocked high, soulfully staring at the bread-bin. Chita will too but not to quite such an extent though now if I say to her 'Where's Janus?' as he can't hear us when we call, she goes first to the kitchen to see if he is watching the bread-bin. If he isn't, she goes to my study where he may be sprawled out in peace, being an old man looking for some sanity in a house where TV sets make funny pictures, and people move pointlessly around answering 'phones and doorbells, getting in an old dog's way; or else he has gone to see if Chia left anything on her plate and, as the door opens the wrong way for him, is leaning forlornly against it, waiting for someone to rescue him.

As he gets older he loses himself round the house, doing the oddest things; hunting hopefully for crumbs, we think. The cat might have left some; we might just have taken a sandwich to the bathroom (not our usual habit, but a dog can hope) or maybe I dropped a packet of dog biscuits when I brought them in from the car. He searches the field with the same kind of anticipation, reminding me of Pooh who always wanted a little something to eat.

Puma adored brown bread too, and when she became blind would put her paws on the draining-board so that she could get her nose near enough to the bread bin and sniff and make sure the bread was actually there. I had to be very careful to isolate her from the other dogs and make sure she had her share, or she lost it to Chita who is very fast and who doesn't eat her food, she inhales it; in one long swallow. Biscuits go down whole. I never know why she doesn't have agonizing indigestion but she doesn't.

It is also necessary to watch that you don't lose half your hand when you give Chita a biscuit as she is over eager, over enthusiastic and more alive than any dog I know. 'Quick, quick, quick,' is her one cry as she races to the 'phone, races to the door, and has to be stopped and steadied. 'Slowly girl, slowly. Steady now, steady.' I train her every time and she is slowly improving, but greed may take over, or sheer eagerness.

I will have the word *steady* blazoned into my brain, I suspect, long after Chita has left us.

'Steady, little girl. No hurry.'

'Try telling that to the marines,' says Chita's expectant little body.

I try to check her, try to anticipate her but she is so fast that at times I get caught out still.

Recently she had what was possibly a bee-sting in her ear; or grass seed. She had a violent allergic reaction and tremendous earache, and our son and his wife and three babies arrived at the same time as her pain, which was far from convenient. We had a very typical Chita drama.

She did not seem to be in agony but she obviously needed treatment so the next morning I left the family to cope and drove the ten miles to the vet. He took one look and said she needed an immediate operation to clean out what he thought could be an abscess deep down. Being Chita, who does not like being left anywhere and is far from happy without me, I was to stay with her, go shopping while she was under the anaesthetic and come back and pick her up to take home.

Chita had her sedative and I put her in the car while it took effect. It was a hot day, so I put her lead on her, fastened her to the handle of the door and opened the hatchback and put her to collapse as dogs should do.

Chita was determined not to collapse. She was going to stay bright and alert and bark at birds, cats, other dogs and people, so I sat with her, telling her she was feeling sleepy and must lie down and be quiet and sensible. She was not convinced. The surgery was still on and there was a lot of coming and going.

Finally she decided she was actually dopey and would behave as other dogs behaved and curled up sleepily. I went in to find one of the nurses to help me carry my now supine little bitch in. 'Can't move,' Chita said. 'Legs won't work.' Her eyes looked at me. 'What's happened to me?'

Out came the nurse with me.

Chita took one scornful look at us, and jumped out of the car. She did stagger once on the way in; but she had made a remarkable recovery from being sedated. It was some time before she went right under.

It was then I remembered we had a club display next day and Chita was the jumping star. There was no way she was going to be fit enough to do anything, and while she was being operated on, I went shopping and then came back and made contingency plans for her part of the display. Two other dogs could stand in, though neither was as experienced as she.

I took her home. She had had her ear attended to and had tablets to get the swelling down, but she was in pain and she was going to take some time to heal; the sting had done a lot of damage and had abscessed. Luckily there was no perforation of the drum.

I spent the day guarding her from the babies who wanted to see her 'poorly' ear. She was still very much under the influence of the anaesthetic and quite content to be left in her bed, barricaded round by dining-room chairs to keep small fry away.

'Could she have a meal,' I had asked.

'She wouldn't want it.'

Our vet had plainly forgotten what she was like. 'Whatever you do, don't let her jump,' I was warned when she was spayed. Ten minutes after coming out of the anaesthetic she was up on the dining-room table (plainly the anaesthetic had addled her brain as that was the first time ever) shouting very rude things at a cat that had unwisely decided to wash itself outside the window. Neither of us had ever seen that cat before.

Chita got out of her bed, after her ear operation, staggered into the kitchen and sat and looked at me.

'Janus is being fed. Chia is being fed. Why aren't I being fed?'

I gave her a mini-meal.

'More, please. I'm starving.'

In the end she had her usual meal and I waited for the consequences. There were none.

I got up in the morning to find Chita already up, with her paws on the low window-sill still watching the cuckoo, who to my annoyance had decided to sit outside the room where the dogs slept and declaim non-stop, at about five-thirty in the morning.

I took her into the garden.

'My ear doesn't hurt. Watch me being a greyhound,' her body said, and she took off at speed round the garden, stopping briefly to go over her scale for fun, take in the hurdle and then roll on her back before speeding off again.

'Ear doesn't hurt. Feel marvellous.' She couldn't have said it more plainly.

I rang the vet.

'Oh, let her do her part; she doesn't even feel pain,' he said. She does, but not for long.

She put on a very creditable display that afternoon and I laughed when, as she went over the nine-foot long-jump, some knowall in the crowd announced loudly 'That doesn't impress me. They starve them for a week and they do it for titbits, poor dogs.'

I thought of the meal she had had the night before when she ought not to have had anything. I have yet to meet a dog you could starve for a week! They are far too demanding for anyone sane to deny them food. Chita would scream the house down if I denied her her supper – even after an anaesthetic!

It is easy to see at this date that a lot of the trouble I had in the early days with Chita stemmed from her insatiable curiosity. Like the elephant's child, she had to know. What was round the corner? What was that thing? At one trials that rapidly turned into tribulations, she had to do a twenty-yard 'sendaway' running away from me in a straight line and then being dropped when I called 'DOWN'.

I was standing facing a large tree, which was my

marker. To my right, at an angle of ninety degrees was another large tree, on which hung a tyre on a rope, obviously used as a swing by children.

I lined Chita up and sent her to her mark. She had had her eyes on the tyre for some time. Out she went to the tree with the swing on it, inspected it, ignored every call I gave her, and when satisfied that she knew exactly what it was, which was a tyre on a rope, she came back and lay down at my feet. No marks at all.

So I practised sending her out with things all over the place. She does fine till she sees something she has never seen before and then she goes off to investigate. Once she has satisfied herself, back she comes happily. I try again – and again – and again!

She also has a sense of territory that is beyond that of most dogs. All dogs guard their homes; all guard the car, and bark if anyone goes near it. The car is part an extension of home and part master's property and personally I want my car defended. I would be furious if it was stolen with the dogs inside! So if they do bark I don't stop them immediately.

Chita does not allow dogs on her patch unless she has been very firmly told 'this dog is visiting us and you will please behave.' Then she is the perfect hostess. And Janus is the perfect host. Both allow visitors' dogs in the house, so long as the dogs themselves behave. Janus never would allow my son's dog in, but as that one had a habit of coming in and cocking his leg to show he was boss and not Janus, it wasn't surprising, especially as Janus was not allowed to cover the marks. He had to put up with it and I tried to clean away the smell. The two of them once enlivened our Christmas dinner by having a fight under the table. After that the other dog couldn't visit us. He is now no more; he was a very dominant dog and ended up in disgrace.

If we are walking, and a dog rushes at us, Chita runs at him to see him off. She has been taught to drop on command so I drop her fast and the other dog, shattered at his reception, makes off. We continue on our way.

*　　*　　*

That is all very well now, but it wasn't when she was younger.

My first inkling of what was to come occurred in Liverpool. I did mention in *Three's A Pack* what chaos she caused, but I didn't then have the courage to confess what actually happened, as I felt it would make people think the dogs right out of control when they weren't, in fact.

The older dogs were triggered always by the puppy. I read that if you have one dog, to control it you need to react three times as fast as with a child; you must react very fast indeed. With two dogs you need to be nine times as fast as with one; and with three dogs it's about twenty-seven times as fast as they set each other off. They do act as a pack at times. Most of the time they are family dogs, behaving perfectly and then something occurs that means they are just dog, and you can have problems.

This particular incident happened almost four years ago and I don't mind confessing to it at this late date as I now know very well it was by no means my fault. It could happen to anyone with a dog, so recounting it might well help keep other dogs alive, as no dog is one hundred per cent perfect. Nor is any human!

We were to sign books at a children's bookshow. It was a huge show, in the Cathedral crypt. I started badly, with Chita yelling she needed to go out in the middle of the Liverpool tunnel. To help matters they had just decided to change the one-way system. I can get lost in any town and have done on a number of occasions, but this one was incredible. I could see the Cathedral; but I couldn't reach it. No matter how many one-way signs I followed, it remained tantalizingly out of reach till I felt like Alice who had been trying to reach a certain hill, and as fast as she got there it removed itself.

I stopped by a taxi rank, produced my press-card, told the driver I was to sign books at eleven; (I use the card about once in a blue moon; obviously this was a blue moon occasion). 'Please could you lead me to the Cathedral?'

51

He had problems as he didn't know the new one-way system either and as it turned out he led me to the wrong side of the Cathedral. I parked on a piece of waste ground at the end of a narrow lane that led to the four-lane highway. The lane was a good three hundred yards long, the road well away, and the Cathedral appeared not to have an entrance. I locked the car and explored, finding the main doorway and the Father who was to meet me.

He came back to the waste ground with me, as we had to drive halfway round Liverpool again to get to the right side of the Cathedral and park my car in the right place. He was sure I would never manage it. So was I.

I walked the dogs on the waste ground, very carefully, on the lead, one at a time. Puma was angelic; Janus had a good sniff round but behaved. Puppy came out, aged sixteen weeks, a minute and appealing little object who looked up at the man in his long skirts, with adoring eyes, and behaved herself like a lamb; and then, just as I put her in the car, removing her lead, and was about to lower the hatchback, a stray black dog appeared, from nowhere, behind me and barked at my dogs.

Out leaped puppy and took off, and the big dogs followed, knocking the hatchback against my forehead. I saw stars, tears filled my eyes and I wondered if I was about to be sick. It was remarkably painful. The priest was very anxious, mainly about me, as he knew little about dogs; then we watched in horror as the four dogs fled across the four-lane road – brakes squealing, hooters sounding, and people shouting, the dogs well out of reach of my voice or me. Finally the dogs vanished into a maze of little backstreets.

I sat on the open back of the car, shaking.

'What are you going to do?' I was asked, sympathetically, after the priest had assured himself I wasn't badly injured; merely a bit dazed.

I didn't know. I picked up three leads.

'Cry, I think,' I said. 'Please pray.'

I walked towards the road, knowing my dogs were

probably dead by now; visualizing huge headlines: 'Author's dogs cause multiple pile-up in Liverpool. Many dead.'

I saw three happy dogs pelting towards me on the wrong side of the road and there was nothing I could do. I wasn't even near enough to tell them to stay where they were and in any case pup was far too young for games like that. Big dogs on their own would have stayed; not little one, only four months old, only sixteen weeks in this big wide exciting world. Only just beginning her training.

I turned my back. I couldn't look.

The noise of braking and shouting repeated themselves and I wished the earth would open and swallow us all up. Luckily neither time were there any bangs. Everyone drove marvellously.

A nose nudged my knee. Three dogs wagged happy tails and grinned at me, panting.

'Saw that one off,' said little Miss Self Importance, full of herself. 'Won't stand any nonsense from other dogs. Good girl, aren't I?'

I was with a priest. I restrained myself from saying extremely rude things to my dogs, and put them in the car, fastening them inside it by their leads. There was no way they would be free to leap out in future. It could cause death to more than the dog, and it didn't do my peace of mind any good either. I was still shaking when we parked the car and went into the Cathedral.

That afternoon I had to talk to the children.

The Father who had been with us was on the other side of the room.

'Do your dogs ever do naughty things and let you down?' asked one small boy. 'Mine is very naughty.'

'Sometimes,' I said, not going to confess that only that day I had had the fright of my life.

I thought I saw a small twinkle come and go in my fellow sufferer's eyes.

That night I wrote off and ordered one of Mrs Cudd's Barjo crates, and for those whose dogs do leap out like that and are either too young or too stubborn to be taught, I can recommend them for total peace of mind.

We did have one small problem with that. Chita can't be caged or kennelled. She has suffered all her life from claustrophobia. She wouldn't stay in the crate with the door on, as she screamed and tore at the wire, but she would stay in it with the door off, a benching-chain, which people use to chain their dogs to show benches, keeping her from leaping out when I opened the hatchback. Yet oddly she loved her puppy pen. That was her den and she'd ask to be put inside it. It was a very big pen.

Now, three years later, it is hard to remember we had to crate her. The cage is constantly being lent to other people in the dog club to save their dogs from death. Chita now lies down when told and does exactly as she is told. She is tied when I'm driving, for our safety.

It is Janus in his old age who needs the benching-chain. It gives him plenty of freedom, but being deaf he doesn't hear me tell him I don't want to drive with him sitting on my shoulders. We did have a dog-guard but one night I did an emergency stop, just after Puma died, and the guard fell on to me and the dogs came forward, one landing on my head and the other over my shoulder on to the steering-wheel. Luckily no harm was done, but I decided it was far safer to have no guard at all.

When we first moved, before I bought Chita, we had a large kennel built to take the dogs. The place was not yet fenced and there is two acres of it. The kennel had a big compound round it. I found out fast that to try and put Chita in confinement was to ask for trouble; she spent all her time trying to escape, screaming so loudly that I was sure the neighbours must think I was engaging in all kinds of peculiar practices. Chita is noisy; she tends to exclaim if she sees something unusual and if left on her own shouts that she is being neglected, come quick, don't like it here, want *you*.

People look at her if I have to tie her at Trials and go

into a building, obviously wondering why on earth I have never trained her to stay quietly tied up. The answer is that she has longer endurance powers than I have over that and since I can avoid it, provided I know what is likely to happen, I don't do it. She gets herself into a state of total panic. It isn't naughtiness; it's plain terror, a fear of being abandoned, or something very like it. She does it even if held by people she doesn't know, as one of the letters in the last chapter shows.

I have tried and tried and tried and tried to train her to be sensible about being tied up, which is the story of much of my life with this particular dog. She sat in a cat cage as a tiny pup, but it always had the lid open, except when, very briefly, I went into a shop. Usually I carried her with me.

In the end I had to waste so much time trying to make her endure being kennelled I decided it was easier to train her to a very high standard to behave herself than to shut her away, and sold the kennel and its outer fencing to someone with dogs that don't mind being put into confinement.

On one occasion my car broke down while I was visiting friends who have boarding kennels. My friend's husband offered to put it right for me and the dogs were taken out and put into a very large kennel, all three together. Janus and Puma lay quietly, amazed, while Chita went into a hysterical fugue. After ten minutes screaming I went to get her; her nose and mouth and paws were bleeding as she had tried to tear her way out. She hates all small spaces, except the car; that is home, where she has her bed, and where I also travel with her. She isn't shut away from me. She will sleep happily at night in her bed, but the room is large, and Janus is there too. I don't know if she will consent to sleep alone when he is gone. And now he is eleven he is not going to last all her life, if she has a normal span.

The second time she was put into kennels was extremely funny . . . afterwards.

I have gone each year, since 1969, to a police headquarters to present a cup for police dog work. Now we have moved it is no longer an easy journey, so I am invited to stay overnight. On this occasion, as Janus was rheumaticky, he was to sleep by my bed, and the bitches were to be put in a portable kennel brought to the back door of the house I was staying in. My host and his wife had two dogs, so I was warned, once we were in bed, not to wander just in case they guarded the house. They were collies, not police dogs.

The police dogs were in kennels just beyond the back gate.

I went to bed, having put Chita and Puma together in the kennel. It was enormous and I did not expect trouble.

I listened to Chita; I was not sure if she was actually charging at the door, eating the wood, or just screaming in tones that grew more and more hysterical. I listened for an hour, hoping she would exhaust herself and settle. It was late as we had been talking. Everyone else slept on the other side of the house and no one appeared to be bothered, but I knew that next-door could hear her and they had a new baby.

Another dog began to howl. In no time at all all of them would be joining in and I would be a very unwelcome guest. I hesitated, wondering whether to knock on my hosts' bedroom door but I didn't want to disturb them, and when I put on trousers and jersey over my pyjamas and crept out, there was no sound. Everyone was asleep. The two collies downstairs were pacing, and Chita was now beyond sense. Even talking to her wasn't going to work. She was screaming and hurling herself against the kennel door which would probably fly open any minute. I would have to risk the collies refusing to let me through.

I told Janus to be quiet, and hoped he wouldn't start getting in a panic himself and either bark or scratch at the door to join me.

I shut him in and crept downstairs; the stairs of course creaked and I felt like a burglar. Luckily it was a dry night. The two collies greeted me with obvious

56

relief, and came to be stroked. 'Do shut her up,' their expressions said. They both looked haunted. She meanwhile had changed her protest from a banshee wail into a keening yodel.

I went outside.

I had two leads. Puma was crouched at the back of the kennel looking as if she too were haunted. 'For heavens sake stop her.' Chita saw me and shut up. I leashed them, and crept down the garden path into the big yard. It was pitch dark and I had no torch. My car was in the garage and I prayed the garage wasn't locked. Past the police dog kennels. Not a sound, though normally they kicked up an awful din. I thought they had probably been shocked into silence; and the silence was blissful. Chita was in a terrible state, and obviously had been in a blind panic, but she became calm now I was there. I put both bitches in the car and sat with them till Chita settled. It was rather like putting a teething baby back to sleep. She, however, was nearly three years old.

I opened the windows partway, and locked the car. The garage was enormous and airy. I lowered the door and went through the kennels, down the path, had a word with two tail-wagging collies, and crept into bed and fell asleep.

There was a knock on my door early next morning. 'Joyce.' A hissed whisper. I woke up. 'Yes?' I called, wondering if I were being brought early morning tea.

'I don't know how to tell you. The kennel door is open and the bitches have escaped.'

'They're in the car,' I said. 'I'll be down.'

I told them of my night's adventure. They hadn't heard her. They were on the other side of the house. 'No dogs barked?' 'Not one.' I went outside and every dog gave tongue! I took the dogs for a walk and came back to breakfast and a day's tracking. I have never tried to kennel Chita since.

I don't know what I would do if she had to be kennelled. She has so much determination and will-power.

Even now she will try disobedience.

'Chita, away.'

And I point to my right, wanting her to run out fifty yards, away from me.

She has a small and very cheeky elf-face, an extremely pretty, an extremely expressive little face. She is foxy in appearance (don't get me wrong; I love foxes' faces). She has a dark muzzle, is beautifully marked, has large erect ears, a bit like bat ears, slightly out of proportion to her head, which is as dainty as the rest of her. Her eyes are dark, with a number of expressions, one of which is extremely old-fashioned, a considering look, as if commenting on human absurdity. Her forehead is marked with dark lines, that sometimes give her a slightly comical worried air, like a housewife who can't quite balance her budget this week.

She looks at me with that quizzical expression.

'To your right? That's what *you* think.'

And off she speeds to my *left*, catching me out, and drops at the end of her run before I tell her to, with a tremendous air. 'So what are you going to do about that?' It's very difficult not to see this dog in human terms sometimes.

'We are going to do it right, my lady,' so up I go to her, do some quick heelwork to make her remember her manners, and start again. 'Oh, if you must.' And she does it perfectly, but I never know when we compete if she will behave.

People who have never met dogs like her can be scathing, but I met a man who knows a great deal about competition and has been in it longer than most other people.

'I had a bitch just like that,' he said. 'Mine gave me two championship certificates early in her life and made me wait ten years for the third to make her a champion.'

I laughed, but it's not funny! It's not too bad if you have a lot of dogs and can show that some of them do well, but when your reputation rests on a couple of dogs with a zany sense of humour, the pair of them, then people are apt to misjudge. I am tempted to take out some of the club dogs I help train; they would do me proud! But my pair give me a lot of fun and fun is what dogs are really about.

Training Chita can be fun, but can provide unexpected hazards. I was teaching her one night in our club training hall. I had gone down early to get in some practice before anyone else came as once I start teaching she goes back in the car. I had put a row of chairs down the hall to make an alley way as she didn't always go out on a straight line for her sendaway. She was sent down the line of chairs to the far end of the hall to drop on command. She did it perfectly five times.

One more for luck.

She gave me one of her old-fashioned looks, and with perfect timing, she jumped the chairs into the hall and jumped back again, clearing three feet easily.

'Chita!'

She did it again.

I heeled her round the hall, did a last perfect sendaway and stopped the exercise. A moment later she was behaving again, doing all she was told so faultlessly it was hard to believe she had disobeyed.

Out in the garden I tell her to hurdle.

So she races in the wrong direction and goes over her scale.

We go back and start again. Faultlessly.

The trouble is I am never sure when she will do it, why she will do it or what makes her do it!

Chapter Four

If anyone wants a lesson in the sheer enjoyment of living, they would get it from Chita.

Life is one breathless whirl of excitement. Even a bird on the lawn has to be exclaimed over. 'Look at that magpie. On *my* lawn.' Go out and sniff and see where he has been and what he has done and what he has eaten.

Race up the field and see if there is a stray cat there; check the ground carefully. 'What's been there in the night? Fox? Hedgehog? Weasel?' They all may visit. If the fox comes he may leave a bone behind him; or a spill of feathers where he has killed; or once a dead hedgehog that had obviously been his night's victim, killed by biting into the soft underbelly.

She does the same things on Miss Marchel's field when she is released from her tracking harness. There are always the remains of kills there; usually feathers, which have been plucked and left as telltales, sometimes half a small carcase of a bird that fell victim. Overhead soar hawks; sparrowhawk and kestrel. On the ground there is scent of pheasant and partridge; every hummock needs to be carefully checked; every blade of grass has some story; some memory, some telltale, and she noses it gently, her eyes half closed, taking deep sniffs. 'Hmmm, I know that smell. Smelt it last week in the big field behind the house. And that's the same as the smells on our grass when that prickly thing has been by; don't like that prickly thing; it hurt my nose and I squeaked.'

Goodness knows if she can think like that, or think at all, or if her brain is a computer of smells, analysing them, checking them one against another; as she must, or how does she know she must follow my footsteps, even when I walk over ground the cattle have fouled extensively for days?

I watch her as she circles the field, her nose down, no longer racing fast, but thinking, identifying, considering, perhaps stopping to look up at me and try to tell me what delights there are on the ground if only I would get my nose down too.

At last she is tired and comes to lie at my feet as I sit against the wall, savouring the rare summer sunshine. She is so much part of my life now.

She comes up the field when I go for the post. If the postman and his van are at our gate, which is a long way from the house, she sits and stays while I talk to him; being a good girl. If it is a stranger at the gate I let her bark and guard me. She knows the difference. She sits watching me. 'Can I carry the letters please?' If there aren't too many she takes them all, being terribly important about it. Working, no time to play the fool now. She walks sedately beside me to the house and comes in and hands me my mail and then goes to her bed, knowing the routine.

Janus comes up later to do his share and carry home the newspaper, which reminds me; it's probably still in the box; time for his walk up there, and his day's job, which he will not yield to Chita. He now forgets he is carrying it though and may drop it on the path as he sees a cat or a bird and takes off, his old brain not quite meshing as it used.

He comes back.

'Sorry, can I have the paper again,' and he takes it from me and goes on proudly, with that wonderful retriever carriage, his tail beating the air, his body, every inch of it proclaiming that he is a personage. Indoors, he no longer hands over; he drops the paper on the floor and runs to the kitchen and barks at the bread-bin; his reward.

In the house, Chita may be lying on the ground, or she may be posing for the photographer who isn't there, sitting on the settee bolt upright (strictly forbidden and well she knows it), but she looks so gorgeous I take time to tell her to get down. She is erect, ears pricked, body tense, tail hanging down in a direct line with her spine, looking out at the field, her back to me, rigid with concentration.

She may be watching the cock pheasant, who has his own ideas about territory and dignity, and is quite unaware that he looks anything but regal scrabbling on the compost heap; she may be watching the heron sail in and land; she may be watching our owls.

Our owls are barn owls and being Anglesey owls, they aren't entirely nocturnal, and, oddly, the birds don't mob them. Maybe they only eat mice and voles and the birds know they are safe. Owl One came regularly for some years, always sitting on the posts that we had so kindly put in for his express benefit. We came to regard him as part of the scenery, perched there, swivelling his head round, watching the long grass, occasionally flying down to pounce and feed.

He would be there at teatime when I drove home, and would stare at the dogs who stared back. He ignored them. They never knew quite what to make of him.

Then one day Kenneth said that the owl was injured. His wings had blood on them. I found my telescope and looked. He wasn't injured; he was wearing two bright orange plastic discs labelled G. He didn't like them much and was trying to preen them out. He gave up and flew off and I wondered if he were unbalanced; he didn't seem to be flying as freely as he had.

He came daily for weeks. I checked the G and watched him.

Chita watched him too, from the sitting-room window, turning her head to see if I had seen him, aware she shouldn't be sitting there, climbing down and coming to me for forgiveness and a moment later forgetting completely, desperate to see out again, sitting there like a small statue, so still she doesn't seem real, her beautiful coat shining as if it were polished. She gleams as she stands in the sun.

Then Owl G vanished and for some weeks no owls were seen. I thought perhaps the nestlings were hatched and he was hunting near home.

One morning a larger whiter owl came and perched,

not on G's roost, but on a post further down. I took the telescope and there on her wings (though it could be his, as even the markers don't know) was the letter E on white, smaller discs.

I puzzled about my marked owls for days and then one Sunday I had an invitation to tea; we were to pass by the Penrhos Nature Reserve. I went in to ask Ken Williams if he knew who was doing the survey. We parked by a blue mini which annoyed both dogs immensely, as on it was a displaying peacock. Just the sort of thing you expect to see standing on a mini.

Chita told it off; Janus told it off.

I moved my car.

I found out who was doing the owl survey and rang them up. Both Owl G and Owl E were nestlings last year, marked by the survey. Owl G must then have been a newcomer as we have had at least one owl ever since we moved and he was smaller than Owl One. I don't know enough about their territory, and nor does anyone else, it seems.

I glance up in the dusk often and the silent flight goes by me, within almost touching distance as Chita and I parade the field late at night; or work in the morning with an owl standing apparently in a grandstand seat enjoying the performance. 'Daft bird,' Chita seems to say as she pauses on top of the scale and looks at it.

The scale, at six feet, gives her a splendid view, and once she is on it nothing else matters. One day she was practising and suddenly the bucket of a mechanical digger in the field next door came level with her as she topped it. She paused. 'Oh, that thing,' her body said and she went down and dropped when I ordered her 'DOWN'.

As she came back over the scale, the driver of the digger appeared over the hedge standing on his seat, fascinated by her performance; she looked into his face with apparent scorn and continued. 'Go away, can't you see I'm busy?' was her air.

He laughed and we held a slightly odd conversation at the tops of our voices above the noise of the digger while Chita, off duty, flattened a few odd molehills and then discovered we had had a rabbit through the field. She tracked it, and came back.

'Are you going to talk for ever,' her body asked me, and the man laughed again and went about his own affairs, and now she was uninterrupted by people who could be such a nuisance she went over her scale properly, intent on doing it right.

She usually enjoys doing it right and gets impatient when club dogs, less experienced than she is, hold her up on the Agility round, so that she has to wait. She watches as they go slowly and then she races round the apparatus, and given the chance will go round on her own, and if I forget to put her through the pipe tunnel goes back to it. 'I haven't *done* that,' she says, indignation in her eyes. Sometimes if I am not concentrating she goes through twice, as she often does her own thing.

When Puma died, I valued the other two so much more; somehow I had begun to take them for granted, my dogs. I had begun to take the family for granted; but life is unpredictable and we are a very long time dead, and death can come suddenly; even more so today when war can erupt in a moment, anywhere in the world.

A speeding car; a careless step and you are gone. Even bombs can interfere with daily life. It puts everything that happens in life in perspective when those you care about most, both human and animal, have died and left you. Nothing can hurt you now; you have suffered the greatest hurt of all and survived. Everything else is trivial.

You know that the dogs at your side will not live for ever; their time is brief. Janus is coming to the end of his life; if we are lucky he may live another few years but now he is eleven he could go at any time. And that makes him doubly endearing; his clowning, his absurd tail-chasing; it won't be there for ever so look at it now. I treasure the memories. I remember another day. He was standing in the car behind me, watching a flock of sheep coming towards us: we had drawn up, so that the sheepdog could work, and there was nobody about but us. The road was solid with woolly backs and behind them the mountains towered into the sky. The radio for once was playing soft music that I enjoy, and not modern pop. Chita tucked her head against my neck. 'Don't bark dogs, not a sound. Let the sheep go by,' I warned Janus, who was fascinated, ears pricked high. Puma could smell them – she couldn't see them.

They passed, packing the road and cars drew up on the far side of the flock, as there was no way we could drive on till the sheep were out of the way.

I watched Chita's face. She too was absorbed, sniffing the air, her eyes brilliant, her ears pricked; her head was on my shoulder, where it often rests, but not while I'm driving. She tucks against the back of my seat.

There is a notebook in the car pocket, and a pen. I never travel without. We were on our way home from a dog show in Worthing, where my aunts are in a nursing home, and I can visit them when I go to the show, near to my friends. I stay with them. I haven't managed to get there for the last two years but hope to go again next year. It isn't easy to get away.

I could do nothing but wait for the sheep to pass – the soft music from the car radio entranced me and the words came, unbidden:

> A lean black bitch with a white tipped tail
> Was driving sheep in Llangollen Vale.
> The cars all stopped as the sheep went by
> Like fleecy clouds in a summer sky.
> The mountains loomed, clad in leafy trees
> That bowed and swayed in the summer breeze.
> The bitch returned the shepherd's hand;
> A pat on the head and a 'Nell, that's grand!'
> On she trotted, her head held high,
> A waving tail and a gleam in her eye.
> A lean black bitch with a white tipped tail
> Was driving sheep in Llangollen Vale.

The sheep vanished; the road was clear and we drove on. I had the makings of a poem; it needed work. But one day it would be improved and be printed.

Scenes can be captured for ever, preserved for the future, for others to read, and it is always good to look back on something that has been inspired by a moment in time.

The days fly past and we often don't have time to stand and stare, to stop and think and remember. Babies are born and grow up, apparently taking long ages to do so, and suddenly they too are adult and have babies of their own and you wonder where the time went and what you did with it. All too little is enjoyed in the frantic rush of living, of the need to get jobs done, racing through the hours as if there were no tomorrow.

I prefer my country home; the cows can't be hurried; the sheep take their time; the farmers move in tune with the animals and the seasons and though they seem to move slowly they get an incredible amount of work done.

My farmer neighbours' tasks are endless; there are the sheep to move every few days; the fields are used in rotation; they stand empty a few days for the grass to grow and then the cows come in, swinging down the lane, and we grow used to their noses thrusting against the hedge, they are intensely curious and come close to the edge of the field if we have the radio on.

The farmer comes daily from his home about a mile away to check them and bring them water, lugging the now redundant milking churns to the trough, which has to be refilled often, as in high summer the cattle are extra thirsty.

The cows graze the grass to one level; and then they go and the sheep are put on, to crop it close; now we have bleating animals instead of lowing animals and the dogs are more interested, scenting the air when the wind blows from the sheep to us.

Sheep noses thrust into the hedge; the sound of their breathing is a little eerie late at night; nothing to be heard but sniffs and snuffles and a noise as if a number of asthmatic patients were lying in the field. The dogs nose against the hedge and then come in. Night-time is bedtime and the routine is well established, whatever animals are next door.

Opposite our dining-room window the dog moves the sheep daily from one field to another; there they occupy three fields in rotation and there the dog brings them to the farmer; they pass him, and he stands watching for trouble, as each goes by.

In winter he comes daily two or three times with hay as the grass has stopped growing and they need extra feed. Yesterday they cut the hay and it will soon be baled; the tractor working long into the evening.

It is September now and our training starts a new season too as we have plough to practise on for tracking, briefly, as the fields will soon be sown with winter wheat; we have stubble, where the summer wheat was cropped, but there isn't a sale for wheat straw here and soon the fields will be burned and for some time we will avoid them.

Then the weeds grow and we can go back again if the fields aren't sown; and later they will be grassed for the cattle and we can go back when the cattle are out of the fields.

Yesterday I went down to the big field to lay Chita a track; it is the biggest field on the farm and was free. But the cattle hadn't settled in the house field which was too hot for them, without any trees to give them shade during the heat of the day, so that as I went to lay my track the farmer came to put the cattle back in the big field.

The field they had left was too newly fouled, so we went to track in the straw, which is not easy but can be done. There are little beasts under the straw; mice and voles, and creepy insects and they distracted Chita from tracking. I laid her a short track, which she watched me walk and she ran it so fast I could scarcely hold her; she found her 'mouse' and she had her romp and we went back to the car where she settled quietly to relax while Janus had his amble down the lane, his sniff around the hedges and his own bit of elderly pottering fun; after Chita it is very relaxing to saunter with him at a snail's pace, and have time to watch the pigeons flying and see the kestrel hover, and the baby pheasants race through the wood, desperate to get away from the giants who, for all they know, threaten their existence.

Oddly I find I can get through much more work here, and yet have far more spare time; I don't know how it happens as I drive daily and since buying my car five months ago have done more than five thousand miles.

Last night we had a club committee meeting and our host's wife commented that there is more time for their new baby here, where life seems to go more slowly, than she ever had before when they were in a busy town, where the two older children were born.

Yet we aren't lazy. It is now just after nine a.m. and I have been working since eight.

I have an appointment to track with Chita at one-thirty and another fourteen miles from there to sort out the training for next session's dog club classes.

There will be time to pick peas for the freezer; to freeze them, to water the greenhouse plants; to take the dogs for a last walk; time has expanded somehow. Time to stand in the village shop and chat for a few minutes; time to greet our neighbours as they walk down the lane; time to stop on the way and walk the dogs beside the sea, and watch the oystercatchers as they wheel and cry and circle over the water; to see the light changing on the hills opposite; and the wind brush the tips of the waves with white.

Time to work out the plot for my next book, to write to my mother and my aunts; time to watch a programme on TV; time to read, time to think; the days seem to have expanded, as there is also time to cook, and time to play with the dogs, and enjoy them.

Later we will take the car and drive down the lane hoping we don't meet anyone, or if we do, that they will be nearer the reversing places than I. Last night I was lucky as I came nose to nose with the farmer's van; he only had a few yards to reverse; another few yards and I would have had to go back a long way, twisting and turning, avoiding the stone walls, the dogs barking because they can never understand why we go into reverse, and perhaps suspect all kinds of strange reasons that necessitate them guarding me against unknown dangers causing the car to behave so oddly all of a sudden. Or if they do see the other car, they may think it is threatening us, chasing us backwards instead of letting us go peacefully on our way. Goodness knows how a dog thinks, or if it thinks at all! But something triggers its behaviour even when we don't know what.

And that in itself is an endlessly fascinating piece of speculation and no doubt all very unscientific, but often an idea dressed up without apparent reason proves in the end to be valid, while all the careful theories fly out of the window!

Chapter Five

One of our greatest inconveniences here is our kitchen; an old dairy with rough stone walls. We have an island unit and by the time Kenneth is there doing his wine-making and I am trying to feed dogs and cook supper and the cat is yelling that she hasn't been fed for a year, life is a bit fraught; especially as both he and the dogs seem to think that feeding-time and wine-making time *must* coincide. All the menfolk in my family have to *do it now* and can't wait for anything. Chita has the same idea.

As I prefer to do things when I've time, it sometimes makes for hazards.

Dogs expecting food don't see why they should wait either. Chita makes her 'I'm being vivisected' noise and Janus adds his deep bay. 'I'm being starved, never mind what Chita's being.'

Chita has the oddest bark.

Puma and Janus both had deep bays; Janus now, if he gets upset, as an old dog can, will suddenly produce a fretful bark; 'come on, I want brown bread, I haven't had any for at least half an hour,' and that wail brings us to see if he is all right. He is. He is just having a brown bread urge again.

Chita's bark is high, and when I want her to 'speak' she can't do it; she is like a girl being asked to sing, and becomes bashful. She manages a mouse squeak and then a soft whining singsong and then if I continue, as one of her exercises later on is to speak on command, she produces a sort of baying whine which promptly makes Janus bark.

Each day with Chita seems somehow to bring me more understanding; she is an unusual dog in many ways; she is very bright indeed; she has had more problems than most in behaviour, but they have mostly now been conquered and are so far in the past few people believe they occurred. Nobody believes Janus was ever difficult either.

We have one club member who has a dog with some of Chita's past tendencies. She is having a pretty horrible time as the bitch is also dominant and is telling off other animals that come near her. I realized two weeks ago that her owner was getting rather desperate as her dog barked at others and lunged and nobody else's dog did.

So I took Chita in and put her under the table and took the money as people came in. Beside her were two King Charlies, both bitches. I knew that if I didn't check Chita she would lunge, and that one of the King Charlies would either whine or bark for her master to return to her.

Then one of our other men, who has a collie, brought him in, and did not check him, so he also barked, being surprised by three dogs under the table. The result was that Chita barked, and had to be stopped; the King Charlie barked and had to be stopped; and the collie came in barking and had to be corrected and the owner of the dog with problems realized that we all do have the same problem; but having been to dog club for considerably longer than she, we can control it. I think she felt a lot better after that.

I only need to say 'No' to Chita now, to stop her in mid flight or attack, or some other mayhem. It is a great benefit with a dog like her.

But just as we have evolved a routine for her, she has developed ways of her own to alert us to her needs.

She butts my knee.

'Can't wait; hungry now, want it now, now, now, now, now.'

If Chita knew human language 'now' would be her main word. There is no 'later' for her; her eyes are flashing imperiously, her body is poised, one paw raised, reminding me of the foxes I have watched from a hidden eyrie, or even sitting quietly in full view, turning, challenging, staring me down and then trotting off on their own affairs, having said with their eyes exactly what they thought of humans. Not very much.

She finishes her meal fast and squeaks impatiently. Janus drives his plate round the floor yet once again as he is convinced that there is still one crumb in the corner. He licks his chops and turns his head and Chita races to the utility-room door.

'Open it. Quick. Now.'

Janus hangs back, and as I open the door she rushes through and is called back. 'No.'

She knows she must not race through, but she is still Chita, too impatient for living; for experience, for knowledge, too impatient ever to wait.

We go through in more orderly a fashion and I open the back door.

Penny time.

Out races Chita, squats and hurtles in again. She has to wait as Janus has gone out in more seemly fashion and is thoughtfully smelling the ground. 'Weasel went round there, a few minutes ago,' he says. 'I know that one. I saw weasel run.'

'Get on with it,' Chita squeals and butts my leg, then paws my knee.

'Behave yourself, little bitch.'

She sits, and waits, in agony, on pins, every muscle so tense that you know as soon as Janus comes in she will explode into action, rush to the biscuit box and if it isn't out of reach, nose it and spill the lot. I put it on top of the deep freeze. Her eyes reproach me. We are in the utility-room, waiting. The garden door is open. Janus is now at the other side of the lawn, considering. 'Shall I, or shan't I?'

He turns and lumbers back to us and then has another thought.

'I'd better.'

He has to explore the grass and Chita is almost dancing on her tail, she *is* sitting, but only just, and every muscle is quivering. Her eyes stare at me, willing me to give her her biscuits. But if I do, she will bolt them whole, as she never chews them, and then challenge Janus for his. And he will lose one or two as he is too slow and too unwily to cope with this little minx.

When Puma was alive she came out into the garden by herself, had a little walk, and her little private puddle and she had her biscuits outside where neither of the others could get them from her. They were always fed together but never unless I was there as the only time Puma did get upset was if Chita came too near her food. Puma never defended herself from that brash pup, but she did defend her food. And she couldn't see. She had to rely on her nose to warn her the other dogs were too near.

If the 'phone rang while they were eating they all came with me and the bowls were put out of reach. I never allow dogs to feed on their own in case the one that eats fastest goes to the other bowl; that can cause a major fight. Even between two pets that always live together. I knew one kitten that was accidentally killed that way.

So Chita has to wait till Janus is ready and being a sober old man Janus believes in taking his time. Nobody would ever guess that once we couldn't get weight on him, as in spite of the fact that he must have his trypsin added to his food, he is well up to the right weight for his size and in his old age is an impressive-looking fellow. He is not fat, but he has the well-developed ponderous body of the older dog, and moves sedately now.

He comes in, ears pricked, head on one side, a question in his eyes.

'Biscuits?'

Biscuits. But almost before I have them out Chita has rushed at me and is trying to nuzzle more than her share out of my hand and I need my sternest voice.

'What do you think you're doing?'

'Sorry, sorry, didn't mean it, will wait. Will sit, only I can't sit still, you're so slow; want my biscuits.'

I put them down, each dog having to wait for just a second. As I say 'O.K.' Janus starts in a leisurely fashion to chew his up, making a lot of crumbs; Chita has apparently inhaled hers whole, one, two, three, four, five, six, and is about to pinch one from the old man. He curls a lip at her. 'Don't you *dare*.'

'Chita, HEEL.'

She comes away from him, 'heels' briefly, but I give no further command so she hurtles to the other side of the kitchen for the next stage in the daily ritual.

She sits in the centre of the island made by cooker, sink and counters, and stares at the bread-bin.

'My brown bread. *Now*.'

Janus is still eating his biscuits. He mustn't waste a crumb. Purposefully, he licks the floor, making sure that that last precious morsel isn't stolen by the cat who has had her own food in private, as one lick of a dog's tongue will demolish her little bowlful and leave her screaming with rage. Siamese cats do shriek. 'Chita's stolen my dinner again.'

Chita moves so fast she sometimes outwits me and cat.

But now she will come past the cat as she is eating. She licks the empty plate when told she may, but walks by virtuously, looking up at me for approval.

'O.K., it's her dinner, isn't it? She has to eat too, doesn't she?' And she noses into my hand and the moment of danger is past. She knows she has been virtuous; every inch of her body says so. 'Aren't I *good*?'

She dances as we walk on; Chita can't do anything soberly.

She dances by the bread-bin. 'Come on, Janus, do.'

Janus has finished at last and he comes to the bread-bin. No nonsense with him.

He barks. 'Ready for my brown bread.'

They watch me cut a thick slice and at last I remember to halve it and not cut it into three and stare helplessly at the third piece that Puma isn't there to eat. She still haunts us; her bowl is now the water bowl in the car, but her memory is there, seeing her as she waited for her food, and then, impatient for the only time in her life, always put her paws on the

counter to sniff the bowls; 'Janus's . . . not mine.'
Janus has a nephritis diet, since two bad doses of
kidney trouble three years ago; it keeps him very well.
We collect it monthly from our vet, together with his
trypsin for his pancreas deficiency. Visits to the vet
for Chita are mainly for fun as she comes in for
Janus's pills and we talk to the nurses and she sits
watching the practice cats, longing to chase them.
They consider they are dogs and come up to her and
sniff her and she quivers with frustration but knows
she has to sit still.

Both cats are beautiful; big tortoiseshells; one of
them is a hunter and came round the corner with a
dead squirrel in her jaws as our vet was loading my car
with tins of nephritis diet.

He looked at Polly.

'I don't think I'd like to meet her on a dark night!' he
said, as she made off hastily with the grey squirrel,
obviously newly killed, dangling from her jaws.

My cat makes havoc among the mice. I have never
seen squirrels here, though they were a major part of
our Cheshire suburban garden.

Thoughts flash through my mind as the dogs chew
the brown bread. We save thick hunks of crust for
them, which they adore. Puma spent her last day on
earth eating the whole of a brown loaf, being given a
private heaven, as every time she asked for bread that
day she got it; she soon discovered that that day was
different and that whatever she wanted, she would
have.

She walked through the woods, just one dog with
me. She loved being Only Dog. She hunted on her
long line, never being pulled in or called. The line kept
her safe as she couldn't see. She lay close to me
indoors and I spent the day with her, and she had thick
hunks of brown bread, endlessly; the others had
smaller pieces as they couldn't be left out; they
wouldn't have understood. They came to see her after
she died, before she was taken away. Janus sniffed her
and went to his own bed; Chita made an enormous
puddle and spent the day subdued, but both knew she

had gone; neither went hunting for a vanished friend and it was less cruel than having her disappear mysteriously, and for them not to know what had happened to her. Dogs understand death and accept it. Ron Tribe insists on this when he is teaching about dogs – and it makes sense. He first taught me of the need.

The vet and his nurse came through the French window and the other two dogs did not know that they were associated with Puma's dying.

It did not appear to worry the cat at all. She seems to live her own life, in spite of the dogs, and not to relate to them in any way. Though she may tempt Chita to chase her, and land on the mantelpiece, complaining loudly. She will also join in the queue for brown bread, but having been given hers, is disgusted as she doesn't really like it; she just doesn't want to miss out on what is going. She knocks it down to Janus who grabs it fast before Chita can get it. That is one trick that Chita never remembers, as Janus feeds under the window and Chita in the middle of the island unit where I can watch her. For one thing, they mustn't change bowls as Janus has his trypsin on his and can't digest food without it.

Then comes the last and most important part of the ritual. This is often when I am interrupted. Perhaps someone calls, or the 'phone rings or Kenneth wants me for some reason; and the dogs are left stranded in the kitchen without the highlight of their meal.

Cheese.

Neither will come out of the kitchen till that last treat has been given. Even Puma would not leave her post by the refrigerator door if I went away without cutting up those three cubes, and handing one to each.

Janus sits, watching the refrigerator door, looking back at me. 'Come on. Do.'

Chita sits as close to the refrigerator as she can get, butting it with her nose. 'It's in there; can't open the door or I would, come on give it to us; want it *now*.' Her body is so expressive and full of purpose. If I am on the 'phone and it is a long call she leaves the kitchen and appears in the doorway, ears pricked, eyes commanding me to come, 'Now, want it, do put that thing down. I'm waiting; you know I'm waiting.' She commutes between the refrigerator and me, at a fast lope, butting me, running to the kitchen door, looking back at me.

'Do come on.'

At last I am ready and follow her and they watch as the packet of cheese comes out. Janus sits, making a pool of saliva on the floor, Chita circles, impatient, unable to keep still, whimpering softly, 'Get a move on, do, get a move on, please.' She circles again, dancing on the spot, leaping up at my hand, being told 'NO. SIT.'

She sits but is up again.

'Won't she ever give it to us? Won't she ever cut it?' Her eyes glint with impatience.

I have made a mistake again and there are three pieces and I cut the last one in two thinking 'Oh, Puma.' Puma's shade watches me from the corner where she always sat, her eyes brilliant and eager even when she was blind.

No dog lies in her corner now. Once she curled up beside me, at the side of the settee, between that and the wall, behind the door, safe from being trodden on. I can still see her curled there in the evening. The other two dogs have their own places. Once or twice Janus has come to lie with a sigh where his old friend once lay, and I wonder, as he sniffs the ground, if it bears traces of her still, four months later. He lies there for a few minutes, and then goes back to his usual place. In everyone's way in the middle of the floor. Chita never goes to that corner at all. It is taboo to her. Yet we have never stopped either of them from lying there.

Janus barks for his cheese, nudging me, because my thoughts are elsewhere.

Chita butts me, jumps at my hand, just missing it with her teeth; 'Chita, behave.'

It is better to practise her formal competition recall than to offer her cheese without taking due precautions. She never means to bite, but she wants it so badly she may snap and your hands get in the way. Janus, told 'Like a gentleman,' takes it from your fingers, between his lips, very quietly and sensibly though even he, now he is old, has sometimes to be reminded dogs may not snatch.

Chita has to practise and for some reason known only to Chita the only way she can practise anything is as a formal exercise.

'Chita SIT.'

She sits, her eyes on the cheese.

'Chita, COME.'

She knows that one and comes and sits in front of me, skidding to a halt because as with everything else, she comes with speed, racing as if there were no future, as if she has to do it now and do it fast, and break the mile record every time. She puts her brakes on at the last minute and never bumps me, which always amazes me as I expect to go down in the rush.

She sits, her eyes on the cheese.

'Now, nicely.'

And as if she had never dreamed of snatching her titbit from you, her small nose comes up, her eyes look at you, and her mouth takes the cheese so very gently and sensibly from my fingers.

'Clever girl.'

'OK.'

She whirls round in a dervish dance; leaps at my face and licks my chin, rushes down the hall after the cat who has leaped to the top of the bookcase and is shouting that *she* hasn't had *her* cheese.

Chita races back to the refrigerator and Janus lumbers after her, always hopeful.

Another piece of cheese, and this time two small crumbs for the dogs. Cat eats hers safely, high up on the sill, where neither dog can steal from her, as cheese makes every animal forget its manners in this house.

Now the dogs are fed, they know the next part of their routine as I begin to cook for humans; the radio goes on for the news, and the dogs go meekly to their beds, without being told. They must now be quiet and leave me in peace. They curl into their tails and we don't hear a sound from them.

Once the table is laid, they leave their beds, and Janus lies beside his master, who in spite of laying down strict rules about titbits is much more likely than I am to slip something to a dog. Chita curls against the wall, having now usurped Puma's old place by my chair, tucked out of the way. She lies with her nose against my shoes. Occasionally she licks me. At the end of our meal she follows me to the kitchen to see what has been left on our plates, as that is more likely to be her trophy; Janus has to have brown bread again as he can't always digest our food. Chita has no digestive problems these days.

Which is just as well as sometimes she eats the oddest things.

She has eaten potato peelings; and beetroot; she loves grapes and pieces of banana; she always hopes there might be an odd potato left, or a piece of pork crackling; she enjoys onion skin; she once took a piece of turnip that dropped on the floor when I was cutting it: that she tried to eat about ten times, but gave up and left it on the rug in disgust.

She has never achieved Casey's dexterity. Casey was Chia's brother. He died three years ago. He would race off with a bag of doughnuts and leave it on the landing, untouched; he once carted a beetroot, fortunately uncooked, up to the spare bedroom. He also brought in a live mole that lost itself behind the deep freeze and caused a tremendous upheaval. I managed to trap it in the dustpan, holding it with some difficulty with the brush, and released it into the bank beside the garage.

I have never seen anything drill into the ground so fast as that mole; he was gone within seconds.

The cottage we live in has been added to in so many directions by so many people that even our visitors get lost. Chita doesn't get lost, but she can get trapped as not all the doors open when she wants them to. We had to change the door handles on our outside doors as little madam let all three dogs out; and since we can't see our gate and dogs might guard when they shouldn't, I don't let them out unless I am with them. Chita could also scale the wall. The need to go with them has an extra bonus as it ensures I get plenty of fresh air too, and more exercise than I might otherwise, as typing is sedentary.

Chita, if I am alone in the house and not too busy, spends her time making sure that we are free from invaders. The stray tomcat, who cries round our house and can't be tempted for food or petting, annoys her immensely. He marches through our garden and may sit under the window and stare at Chita who barks back in rage.

'Go away, you. This is *my* territory.'

Once she was racing up the field full of pleasure at being free. I had thrown her rubber quoit and she was hunting for it in the long grass. Neither of us knew stray cat was there.

He reached up a long leg, scratched her tummy and bolted.

Chita bolted after him. No way was any cat going to do that to her. I called, but she remained deaf. Her mind was on one thing only; on teaching him a lesson. Down the drive and to my horror over the wall which is never allowed and which she had never attempted before.

I yelled to her, but she was gone and just down there was the sheep field. I could have killed that cat. Wretched animal – he haunts us and sprays our doors and even the walls if he can get inside.

I yelled again, 'Chita COME.' Back she trotted and over the wall and sat at my feet.

'Lost him. I've come, aren't I *good*?'

She *was* good; she had come when she was called and there was no way whatever I could punish her for having run away, as that was in the past. She'd think I'd punished her return. But she had to realize that going over that wall was totally taboo. It couldn't be allowed. Even if she were safe with sheep, they were

in lamb and might run from her; might drop a lamb
early and that lamb would be bloody and the scent of
blood would be more than any dog could resist. It
would go up and sniff; and blood means food to a dog.
And that would be the beginning of the end.

I heeled her to the house and fetched her tracking
line.

Up to the wall by the gate. It is far lower than her
scale, but up to then all the dogs had respected our
boundaries, except for Janus who had once discovered
that if he shook the gate hard enough he could rattle
the bolt loose, get out and go walkabout. He is that
kind of dog so I have to watch Janus all the time and the
gate now has a special reinforcement on it to foil him.
People leaving my gate open don't get invited again as
I won't have my dogs free in the village, where they
could get run over. We live next door to farmland
where they could harass stock. The farmer has as
much right to my consideration as I have to his.

So I put Chita on her long line, and threw the quoit
over the wall. As she raced to get it I shouted
'CHITA, NO, COME,' and tugged on the line. It took
about twenty throws before it dawned on her that I
meant it; that that wall was something she must not
jump over; and now she will come up to the gate and
sit beside me and not even look at it.

All the same I don't tempt providence; not with
Chita.

Janus now paws at the gate hopefully and then
bumbles back to me.

'Won't open. Can we go for a walk?'

Walking in the village is no fun as too many dogs
run free. I could take Puma as she never threatened
another dog, but Chita won't stand being attacked and
attacks back and I don't like fights when dogs are
about. People can get bitten.

I discovered last week that Janus, when a young dog
rushed up to him friskily, now just sits of his own
accord. The other dog is baffled, and walks on – and
we proceed in peace. Old dogs get very wise. We were
on a course with about twenty-five other dogs. He did

81

it a number of times. People thought I had told him to. I can't. He can't hear.

So we go for walks in distant places where other dogs don't roam and where sheep aren't likely to be found; and I know we are safe from hazards. The dogs can do as they like then, and they happily hunt the sand dunes, or chase hopefully after distant birds, safely controlled on the thirty-foot line, and get all the exercise they need.

My favourite wet day exercise for Chita is to go to the dunes which are very near a fast main road, put her on her long line, and throw her quoit to the top of the dune; up and bring it back over and over. It takes about twenty throws to tire her out as she races up at speed and comes down even faster, enjoying every second of it.

'Cor, I've had enough,' she says at last, panting, and I take her back to rest and walk Janus more soberly; he finds all kinds of scents and investigates them ponderously, taking his time. Nothing hurries Janus now except, very occasionally, a sudden desire to be young again, and race after a toy which I have thrown. On some days he just looks at me. 'I grew out of that stage long ago; you are tiresome' his eyes seem to say.

Then he reverts to puppyhood, and dances for me; 'Come on, I'm young today. Let's have a game then.' He may come when I throw my car keys; he will come if he thinks Chita is being favoured; occasionally he will take something from her mouth and she will let him, giving a token tug, as he races off with it and she comes to me.

'Did you see what he did? Anything in your pockets I can look for in the long grass?'

I throw something for her and she races in and pounces, grabbing it in her teeth and racing back, at top speed, to skid to a halt and sit, pushing her face at me. 'Take it then; come on, quick, quick, quick.' I laugh and take it from her and praise her and she preens.

Most dogs are affected by the wind; some by the full moon. Chita being Chita, who does everything with five times as much zest as most animals, being so full of health and high spirits, almost literally 'bursting her skin' is affected by both wind and the full moon. If both occur together I need to watch her all the time, as she goes quite loopy!

I found out early in her life that on windy days she was almost impossible to manage; if I took her to club she played up all the time. So do many dogs, and children. Nothing dangerous; she isn't dangerous; just full of mischief, sparking at other dogs, leaping out to say 'boo' I suspect, but other dogs and their owners don't like it.

Wind is a hazard of our lives here. Very few people in towns realize just what it does to those in the country. Our land is surrounded by trees; trees that creek, trees that sway, trees that scream. When she was small, Chita joined in, yelling her excitement, unable to contain herself, rushing from window to window to look out at the big wide lovely mad world out there, rain lashing down in torrents; and to puzzle over the fierce invisible monster that tore at her fur with unseen paws when she went outside, the wind running like a rogue elephant through the fields.

Wind is something I never mind if Kenneth is at home; if he is on his boat I am as edgy as Chita but in a different way. I can visualize the sea, the giant rollers flinging the boats about with a fine disregard for human life; the yell of the storm as it screams over the white-crested waves, the rocks waiting just off the shore to grind an unlucky boat and kill its occupants. I am no sailor.

Kenneth was on his boat just before the Fastnet race. Luckily he saw the plunging barometer and knew that something very unusual was about to happen and also luckily he was in harbour, and near to home. I did not know he was safe and driving back to me. I listened to the radio, looked at the evil sky and the wicked scudding clouds, and heard the wind that here behaves like a mad thing, racing round the cottage, banging against the pigsty (which is full of logs, not pigs) knocking over Chita's scale as if it were matchwood. It is remarkably heavy for me to lift again.

Chita trots busily round the place, finding her bone and playing with it, unable to keep still. She lies on her back, legs in the air, bicycling fast, much faster than Janus ever does. She rolls ecstatically on her bone, leaps up, tosses the bone and catches it, trots to me to share it, trots round the room, hiding it briefly and discovering it again as if she had never seen it before, a mischievous look on her face. She pushes it under the settee, thrusting it further with her paw so that she will have to work out how to get it out again; the settee is wooden-legged, and there is an eighteen-inch clearance. She lies on her tummy, her tail beating furiously, as intrigued as if she had a rat there, seeking to work out her problem. She can't reach it that way, so she crawls behind the furniture, and manages to get it in her mouth. Then she has to come out in reverse, very slowly, as there is a table on which I keep all my pot plants. It is low enough for the dogs to knock the plants off if they are careless; that only happened with Puma, who couldn't see and sometimes was too close to it. The others do take care.

Gale warnings are part of my life, always. I had not realized that they are not part of other peoples' till we had Roy Hunter and his wife to stay with us. Kenneth, as always, listened to the weather forecasts, as he should have been at sea on holiday but was stormbound. I had a carefully-planned three weeks of visitors so that I wouldn't be alone.

But the weather intervened and we both enjoyed our visitors and Kenneth is still waiting to go to sea! By the end of their week our town-bred friends were aware of the weather.

I rang recently to see how they were, and to my amusement discovered that they too now listen to the weather forecasts and the shipping forecasts, and look at one another and wonder if Kenneth is fishing today, or if he is at home waiting for better news and is galebound yet again.

This summer he seems to have been constantly

galebound. So much so he has just decided to sell his boat. He was to have gone off last Tuesday and I went out, bought food for one, and also bought all the fruit he doesn't like and I do; ending up with, among other things, a mango, a pawpaw and a lime.

I came home, adequately stocked for one, but not for two, to find yet another gale warning and a husband who had come home again, and that I had not stocked wisely at all; our supper was rather odd.

The next day I was due to go and watch an agility display forty miles away, but by lunchtime it was cancelled because of torrential rain. And this is summer! The next day friends were going to the Royal Welsh Show and as I looked out of my window on to streaming fields, the cattle huddled miserably under the hedges, the trees protesting as the wind played games with them, I was glad I decided not to go. The drive through the mountains would be fierce, the rain pouring off the hillsides, the wind catching the car on the moors, the world bleak and desolate.

It was the holiday season and there were campers only a few miles from here; they would have spent a miserable night. The wind played games somewhere on our ground for hours with a loose piece of corrugated iron, that banged like a roll of drums nonstop; by five-thirty Chita was awake and had managed to open the folding door into the kitchen, another of her little tricks that Big Dogs never managed, and had drunk all the water in her bowl, and was soon telling me she can't wait, come quick or there will be floods indoors as well as out.

Knowing Chita, I knew she was right.

I crawled out of bed and down the stairs to find both dogs sitting waiting for me. Janus had decided to get up early today too; 'can't sleep, all that noise, nobody could,' their eyes said as they ran to the window and looked out at the soaked and miserable stray Tom. He bolts when he sees us.

I took four biscuits in each hand and opened the utility-room door on to the back garden. 'And about time too,' Chita indicated with a sigh of relief and raced into the storm, emptied fast and raced back, banging against my hand. 'Come on, done it, biscuit time.'

Janus more leisurely, came in damp, and sat watching me.

'Biscuits? Been good?'

I gave them each their share and went back into the kitchen. It was not quite six; and Kenneth was up making tea, prior to listening to the shipping forecast. I looked at the scudding clouds, at the windows streaming with rain, at trees that were not still for a second. Chita was standing with her paws on the sill looking out in delight. Her ears were pricked, her eyes brilliant, her whole body poised and eager. She even manages to sleep in a tensed position and the slightest sound has her on her paws, looking, head on one side, asking 'What's that? Do I need to do something about it?'

The shipping forecast was as expected. Gales in the Irish Sea. As if we didn't know. Kenneth went back to sleep but I couldn't. I got up and had a bath and listened in amusement to Chita hearing me have a bath.

The dogs sleep in the old part of the house; it's an odd house, which started about three hundred years ago as a tiny stone cottage, with only two rooms and a little passage. It was a farm cottage and part of the pin-money dowry of a wife of a peer who lived in the South of England. His family seemed to own a lot of property round here. Among other properties were the joiner's and the blacksmith's, both now private homes with their former use unrecognizable.

The room the dogs sleep in has been extended to include a dining annexe at one end; it is an L-shaped room, with two doors leading into a big new hall, off which is a passage and my study and a very large lounge, or at least, it's large for a cottage. When we came the first door in the middle of the house was the old front door and still had its yale lock. Unfortunately it didn't possess a key and if we weren't careful we could lock ourselves in the new part of the house and be unable to get back except by going right round to the old part and hopefully finding the other main outer door unlocked. We now have a normal door there!

On the other side of the main room is an archway leading into the old dairy which is now our kitchen. It has rough stone walls and is remarkably inconvenient as if we put kitchen units against them, all we do is provide runs for myriads of mice that the cat can't reach. Hence the island unit, where we are constantly in one another's way. The dogs add to the hazard so that if either of us is in the kitchen and a dog comes in, whoever is there says 'OUT' without even stopping to think and a forlorn animal droops its tail and goes away again. No food this time. Janus now needs a signal.

Janus stays hopeful. 'Can't hear. What did you say? You don't mean *me*. I mean, the bread is there, just by your hand.' The only thing to do with him is to shake our heads violently from side to side. *No*.

He does know what that means, and sighing deeply, he goes away.

The other door leads into the room where the boiler is, and the stairs, and if you turn again, into a tiny passage, you come to the bathroom and lavatory that we built on to replace a corrugated-iron-roofed extremely Arctic lean-to.

If Chita lies close against the door of the room she sleeps in, she can smell me having a bath; or at least, I think that is what she's doing. Her nose is against the door crack and she is taking deep and very audible breaths.

'You're there; I know you are. Come on, I'm all alone.'

Not that she is; Janus and Chia are with her.

The deep breathing continues, getting more agonized and noiser, more demanding, more impatient. I have never heard a dog that could breathe with such eloquence. 'Come on.' Breathing isn't going to work. There is a very faint, almost inaudible whimper.

She whines. 'Chita, *No*.'

Allowed to make a noise, Chita still deafens us and half the neighbourhood and has to be stopped. Quiet, every time; only the trouble is other people don't stop her and I can't be there one hundred per cent of the time and if I feel off-song or am busy or preoccupied, I may not stop her every time either, and the trouble begins again. A noisy animal is irritating. Chia, our Siamese cat, if she doesn't want to go to bed when we do, can be a pest, screaming that it isn't bedtime, nobody loves her, she hasn't had her cuddle, we didn't give her enough food, the stray cat's outside and walking about and there is an owl out there and the moon is bright and why can't she go outside and no we aren't going to sleep, so there. She can't go out as we know of two cats that lost an argument with a fox – and there are foxes.

I go down, have words, and glare at her.

She glares back and then melts, squeezing her eyes at me. She becomes soft and boneless, purring loudly and as I turn to go out of the room, maddens me by a giant leap to my shoulder which I wasn't expecting, almost unbalancing me and sits there, buzzing contentedly. I put her down in her bed and she starts her noise again.

In time, she does settle but on occasion I have to go for a small handful of cat nibbles, to shut her up and let everybody get some peace. By now Chita is sure something is going on and she should be included and if cat has titbits then Janus has to go and sit by the bread-bin and if I am not fast enough, he barks. 'Leave that stupid cat alone and come to me.'

All in all it sometimes seems to take ages to go to bed.

Meanwhile Chita is probably by now on the wrong side of the door, deep breathing again, lying with her nose under it. 'Can smell mistress, know she's there, why doesn't she come?'

In the end I pull out the plug and dry myself and go back to the dogs. Chita greets me as if I have been away on an Arctic exploration for a year. 'Where have you been? Why didn't you come? I do love you, why do you leave me alone; what are we going to do now?'

She trots expectantly to the door. 'Cat left some food. Wasn't smelling you; I was smelling Chia's breakfast. Hungry.' She investigates the plate which has at least two just visible crumbs on it and licks it clean. Janus sniffs it and decides its not worth wasting his energy, and sighs and returns to bed. He hates rain.

I will need wellingtons just to get the post.

It takes me back to another gale two years ago, when Puma was still alive. Puma was the centre of that day's drama.

She had a cyst on her back; Chita also tends to get tiny cysts, which are part of many dogs' lives and don't matter at all. Some stay; Janus had one on his ear flap which did have to come off; but Puma's either went away or burst and none had given any trouble.

This one grew.

It grew to the size of a hen's egg and our vet decided it would have to come out. She went in for the operation which was no problem as he is a splendid surgeon and this didn't seem as if it would be a difficult operation.

It proved more so than he had expected, as he thought afterwards that the cyst had abscessed internally, had ruptured, had put down infective points and these had somehow formed branches of tissue inside. It was like a cancer but it wasn't malignant, though we didn't know that for several rather worrying days.

It had to be cut out and far more tissue had to be removed than we expected. There was a very large hole at the end of the exercise, with several stitches to close it.

This was done about two weeks before our club was to have a match with another club forty miles away. Matches are friendly get-togethers, not genuine matches in this area; just a test against the other club, with little prizes for the winners. They are fun, liven up the long dull winter, and we host our visitors with a party at the end of the proceedings. We ask an outside judge.

On this occasion I had not yet met our judge, who had been very active in the dog world in her day but was now retired. Friends had suggested asking her and I was to collect her. She lives six miles from me, but in the opposite direction to the club hall.

I planned the day very carefully.

I would collect the judge, feed her, and take her over (a matter of eighteen miles by then); I had everything ready, luckily; the prizes, the various items we needed, and I had chosen the teams who hopefully had been practising hard.

The gods as always upset my plans.

It was November, which is not much fun in towns and can be hell in the country. It had been raining for some days. Janus went outside early in the morning and found something distinctly unpleasant and rolled in it. I didn't notice until he came up to me for bacon rind while I was eating my breakfast.

The stink was unspeakable. Whatever he had found must have been very dead.

Appetite gone, I took him into the bathroom and coped; he still stank and ended up sprayed with some rather rich scent I had been given for Christmas, which offended his nose. He walked round with a distinctly unhappy expression on his face.

Chita thought it extremely odd and kept annoying him by going up to him and smelling him, with an air of total disbelief on her face, so that he told her off.

Puma, by now half blind, was in her usual corner.

The weather was increasingly evil. The wind was beyond gale strength and the rain never stopped. I decided there was only one thing to do with the morning and that was to type. At two I would sort out the afternoon's affairs, get everything in my car, and go over and get our judge, so that I didn't rush her as she wasn't a young woman.

At twelve Liz came to say Puma who had had her stitches out the day before was bleeding badly.

I went to look at her. The healing wound must have

irritated her and she had been rolling, as the telltale marks on the carpet told me. I mopped her up, and decided I had better ring the vet.

'Sounds as if she needs stitching again. Can you bring her over at two – and she is going to need an anaesthetic, I think.' Luckily her last meal had been the evening before so she'd only had two biscuits since.

I explained about the match. It meant that I was going to be nearly twenty miles from the judge instead of six and nobody with transport, from the club, was on the 'phone. No problem if I came immediately. I decided, fortunately as it turned out, that I had better change into the clothes I intended to wear, and hope I didn't get bloodstained. I was going to have to drive forty miles instead of eighteen. And the weather was increasingly awful. And I was going to have an anaesthetised dog and what did I do about that?

I had gone without breakfast and I couldn't finish my lunch as I was busy trying to mop blood, which was getting everywhere. Puma was inclined to shake herself and the hole was bleeding quite badly; the wound was gaping again. It had looked so healthy and had seemed completely healed, but the new skin was obviously tender and not up to being rolled against rough carpet. And Puma could never leave an injury alone. She was a pest with any cut or sore, and scratched vigorously.

I left home at about half past one, driving out into weather so wild that the car behaved like a boat in a high wind and the steering felt terrible. Traffic was crawling along, and even with the windscreen wipers on fast the visibility was bad; we crept with full headlights, through a darkness more like night.

The wind increased, which I hadn't believed possible.

As I reached the bridge across the Straits the sky seemed to leap into action and lash itself at us. The traffic stopped; the bridge seemed to swing and I had visions of it breaking and landing us all in the water deep below us; and that would be a remarkably unpleasant way to die.

We didn't know it then but at that moment the new school gym was blown down.

The traffic began to crawl again and I reached the vet. His house was in total darkness. All the lights had failed, and he had had to go out to an emergency.

I was due to collect the judge at five.

The clock crept on; we drank coffee, we mopped Puma and occasionally checked the other two dogs, both, remarkably, asleep in the car. At that stage Chita and Janus could never travel together; they tended to argue. So the back of the car was divided in two by a dog guard that went across behind my seat, and the car was also divided like a police van down the middle. The two bitches always travelled together.

Time began to rush, not creep, and still no vet.

He returned at four and tried to start the generator. A pylon had blown down and there would be no power. The generator wouldn't start and in the end Puma had her stitching done in the light of two big headlamps, all very primitive and unlike his usual very efficient set-up.

I rang the judge and explained and she very kindly said don't worry; the dog is more important than the match and she would expect me when she saw me.

We put Puma in the car under a rug and put Janus and Chita together, which worried me. So did Puma. Suppose she had an adverse reaction to the anaesthetic? There was nothing much I could do. I drove back through wind and torrential rain and came to the judge's home. By then it was almost six.

I was telling her about my day when she said 'Have you eaten?'

She very sensibly had while she was waiting. I had not only not had anything to eat before going to her, but had had about a tenth of my lunch and only a quarter of my breakfast and realized I felt remarkably light-headed and rather sick.

We decided, in view of the appalling weather, I wasn't going to be very safe driving if I didn't stop and eat. We stopped and I had a steak; eaten in a tremendous hurry, worrying about the match. I hadn't been able to ring anyone; I had the judge, the other club had had to drive through the mountains and I hated not being there to greet them; but the Fates had conspired against me and nothing much could be done.

By the time I arrived everyone had decided I had forgotten to come! The teams seemed to have got themselves in a muddle so that one team had five people in it instead of four and I had to decide who to take out; and whoever I chose to ask to stand down was not going to be pleased and I was so tired that I had no energy left.

Also I was worried by the thought of Chita and Janus in the same compartment for two hours, as I couldn't bring either of them in; I was too busy; and Puma was still unconscious.

I sent messengers to her every half hour. She recovered and seemed unconcerned. When I went out to drive the judge home, Janus and Chita were lying quietly and Puma was sitting up, looking out of the window at the rain. It seemed a very long drive back to the judge's house; we had had the match and our food, and the speeches of thanks. The wind was still gusting and the rain was still pouring, and the roads were partly flooded; and there was twenty miles to go.

I left our judge, refusing her very kindly offered drink. I wanted to get Puma into the warm. I had to drive through six miles of narrow lanes, unlit, wet, the hedges masking my view, crawling through the dark, wishing I were home.

Today, as I write, looking out at the rain and wind-lashed fields, is very like that day.

Other days like it come to mind. Coming home from visiting my mother on the South coast, driving through the mountains, with floods every few miles; creeping slowly through water, not knowing how deep it was, horribly aware of notices saying 'Liable to subsidence,' or 'Beware falling rock'; aware that the waterfalls were in full spate, the water crashing down the hillside, perhaps out of control, perhaps due to bring a landslide down on the car.

Driving with the rock face sheer on one side, luckily with a low stone wall, but with odd gaps where a rope and warning flag told how some unwary motorist had crashed through; the mountains bleak and austere and unfriendly, towering above, great screes of fallen rock, bare of all vegetation; pathetic little tents clinging hopefully to grassy slopes, their occupants leaning forlornly against walls, dressed in their rain gear.

The huddled sheep lying under the bushes or under the lee of stone walls; or standing patient, enduring for ever.

Behind me the dogs sleep, oblivious of human worries, of the fact that I am aware of extra hazards, of slippery corners where a car might skid, of lorries bearing down on me, apparently on the wrong side of the road, of the endless curves and corners of the winding mountain road.

Home is far away.

I think of Robert Frost's poem.

> I have promises to keep
> And miles to go before I sleep.

He was riding a pony. At least inside my small capsule I am dry, even if worried by increasingly vile conditions.

Once home after any journey I let Big Dogs out first. Puma, as always, performed fast and ran to the door; 'let me in, out of this weather.' She always hated weather. She was as fastidious as any cat about rain; no matter how filthy Janus got, Puma could come on the same walk and arrive home immaculate, needing only a chamois leather over her coat to return to her beauty.

Janus needs about ten towels and looks a muddy ragbag till he dries out and I can brush him back to looking more like a dog. Even then his coat is soon shaggy again, as if it hadn't been touched. He never does repay me for grooming him, except for brief moments.

And that reminds me of another absurd day.

This was high summer and for once it was a fine day and we were at Rhyl.

The show there is held on the promenade. Not the best of places as the cars are parked a long way from the skating rink, which is where we all end up. Dogs have to be tied to railings if you have more than one and children swing on railings and Puma never did like being tied while I worked Janus.

I left her with someone I knew slightly, who didn't notice her industriously chewing her lead.

I was working Janus in the ring, and called him to me. To my surprise Puma arrived too, holding half her lead in her mouth.

'Which dog do you want?' the judge asked.

Puma had to be held while I finished working but both Janus and I had been put off. I entered Puma in Breed, the only time I handled her in an open show. Somebody had very kindly given me some handling lessons as Breed isn't my favourite type of show. Instead of heeling by my side, Puma had to move out in front of me at a fast pace, and then I had to stand her to look pretty for the judge.

As soon as I got her front paws right she moved her back paws or turned her head and was remarkably unco-operative. My instructor was standing behind me at the rails, hissing.

'Move her front paws.'

'Look at her tail.'

'Get her ears up.'

That was easier said than done as Puma loved me with her ears flat; they were only erect when she was alert; with me they often did lie back and she would look up at me with huge soulful eyes. 'Oh, isn't this fun, just us?'

Puma loved being 'just us', those other wretched dogs elsewhere.

Finally I did get her set up more or less correctly and I think we came out with a second that day.

I went from there to work Janus and sat next to a dear little lady who knew all about dogs and dog shows, though she had never been to one before. She admired Janus. He reminds people of a teddy bear and looks very cuddly and on occasions will let you cuddle him. This was one of the occasions. He yearned at her and she adored him.

'He'll win,' she said confidently.

I laughed. He couldn't, not that day, that was for sure, as one of our early walks had produced not one, but two bitches in season come to the Breed show and his mind was definitely very much on Other Things and he was sniffing the air. 'Coo. Isn't that lovely.'

We worked and my neighbour assured me he had won. It then turned out that she had confused the Breed and Obedience and thought every dog was there for its breed and would only be placed if there were two or more of the same breed; and Janus was the only retriever in Obedience, so he had to be first in his breed.

I never did get through to her I was competing against forty other dogs!

She was very angry when the judge gave the first prize to someone else; and argued that all the dogs who represented only one of a breed should all have a first.

I gave up the argument and took the dogs on the beach.

We had finished for the day.

That proved a mistake as the beach was full of children, the tide was out and there were lovely pools and I didn't realize that the sand suspended there. Dogs went to play with a group of children and everyone had a riotous time. I called the dogs. Home time.

Out they came, both smothered in sand. This was before Chita's day. Heaven knows what she would have done. I now keep off the beaches in holiday time. Dogs can be a major hazard, shaking water all over people and picnics, or puncturing balls.

The dogs shook themselves.

I leashed them. The only way back to the car park was past the show rings. And to cap it all, the judge had just reached the class for golden retrievers and there were rows of immaculate goldies, all groomed till they shone, and there was I, standing well away, with the scruffiest animal you ever saw, his coat plastered against him, covered in sand, mouth open, panting, eyes glinting, obviously happier than many of the dogs in the ring.

As I walked past to my car I heard someone say 'That woman's a fool. Imagine taking a dog in the sea just before putting him in the show ring. No wonder they wouldn't let her enter.'

I sat in the car grinning. Nobody in their senses would ever show a dog like Janus. I once asked a friend who judged goldies if she would give me a show criticism of him.

'Are you sure you really want it?' she asked.

I was sure. We are still friends, but I won't embarrass poor Janus by listing all his faults! Beauty is very much in the eye of the beholder and most non-show people who like dogs think he is gorgeous. So does he, and after all, it is his view of himself that colours his life. As far as Janus is concerned he has star quality. He walks as proudly as any champion and enjoys life, probably, far more.

Chapter Six

One of the major difficulties in writing about dogs is that we all want something different from our dogs and that the word training may cover a multitude of things. What I mean by training probably isn't what you mean!

A guide dog and a police dog both have a kind of training most people would not attempt; it is a long and dedicated process, to ensure a good reliable steady dog at the end of it, and both types of training require special types of dog. The police and the guide dog people choose very carefully indeed, as both need exceptional qualities.

If they don't have them then a long and expensive training is wasted. Many dogs are rejected. They make very good pets, but aren't up to the demanding life required of a working dog.

A farm collie must be healthy and capable of spending long hours outside in the open air. Gundogs have to accompany their owners, must pick up game that falls in brambles, nettles, thick cover, or water; must understand that the game is not for them and bring it in without damaging it; must swim if necessary, scramble over rough ground, through wire and over walls.

Hounds are meant for chasing and worrying. For long runs in the open air in a pack; and of all dogs, a hound is the one I would never, personally, choose as a *pet*, as the instincts to hunt are so strong and so is the pack instinct. Pack dogs are hooked on dogs and not on people, and it is remarkably hard to get the undying affection of one of the hound group to one person, as you can with many other breeds.

Greyhounds, Afghans, Whippets; all adore racing and chasing; they were originally bred for it. The German Shepherds, the Dobermanns, the Rottweilers, among others, are bred to guard, to be trained to attack, and if the owners don't give them enough to do (and that doesn't mean exercise, but using their brains and occupying them) then they get into trouble. Not because they are bad, but because they are not employed.

People sometimes think it cruel to train dogs and don't understand the problems other people may have with their dogs. There is no way I could have lived with Chita if she hadn't been highly trained. Since she has come up to police dog requirements, except for *attack* routines which I won't teach a pet dog, she has become far easier to live with as she knows the rules and mostly she obeys when told. But she couldn't obey till she knew what she had to do; she had to be taught.

If I went into a room full of Welsh people and someone said 'Ysta', I would now know what to do. Those who don't speak Welsh wouldn't. I would simply sit on a chair.

My Welsh is as basic as a dog's as some people in club speak Welsh and I have learned it through their commands! But until the dogs know what SIT means, the dog can't do it. He *must be shown*; so many people expect their dogs to be telepathic and to understand what the owner means when the poor dog hasn't a clue what he is supposed to do.

With dogs like Chita, the training has to be firm; *not* cruel, *not* harsh, but you must *mean* what you say. No use saying 'no' in a 'yes' voice; it doesn't mean no. 'No' must be in a 'Don't you dare' voice; and then the dog understands.

People unfortunately don't always understand about other people's dogs even when they have their own.

I once wrote about taking out Puma and having her paws blistered by something spilled in the road. I got a number of letters saying I should have carried her. On that day I was walking four German Shepherds together, all adult, and had to cross a newly surfaced road to get back to the kennels which were in a cul-de-sac, and, unfortunately, nothing less than a helicopter would have got them there without contact with the road. We'd been on a five-mile circular run and the road had been surfaced during our walk. My correspondents all had tiny dogs.

Recently, when I was talking to a friend about Janus's deafness, she told me of someone who had a deaf dog and suggested I rang her. I did.

One of our problems is waking Janus when he is asleep as he doesn't hear us now. He has to be shaken gently and I am always a little worried lest it startle him into defending himself if somebody strange does it. I wondered if there was any way I could deal with the situation.

'Just pick him up and gently cuddle him, my dear;' said the very pleasant voice on the other end of the 'phone.

'What breed is your deaf dog?' I asked.

It turned out to be one of the tiny breeds, which is very different and when I explained I had a large dog and no way could I lift him gently and cuddle him, she decided she couldn't help. She had very different methods of dealing with her tiny mite; they aren't possible with a hefty fellow weighing well over seventy pounds.

There are other ways in which people fail to understand dogs.

Big dogs play very rough.

Janus and Puma delighted in a free-for-all on the beach. I only allowed this when it was deserted as nobody wants galumphing lumps hurtling past them showering them with water or sand, rushing off with their balls, or even knocking down their children. So I only go on winter beaches.

On this day it was a bright calm day in December; cold enough for your breath to plume. I took the dogs to a distant sandy beach where few people walk and found I had it all to myself. They rushed down to the sea, barked at the waves, raced back to me, rolled over and then began to 'eat' one another.

Janus decided he was going to bowl Puma over. This

was something Puma adored, and she waited for him, standing sideways, as he charged. He rolled her and then took off, and she followed. He lumbered and she moved like a dream and as I watched them both, enjoying the sun and the wind and the emptiness and the sea, a furious voice spoke in my ear.

'You wicked woman!'

I turned and found myself staring at an elderly, obviously retired military gentleman, dressed rather improbably for the beach in beautiful city clothes, glaring at me from hot little blue eyes, his moustache wagging indignantly.

'Why?'

'Setting your vicious Alsatian on that innocent dog. He's hating it.'

That innocent dog at that moment was in fact planning an even more devastating body roll at Puma, and had turned, head down, and was about to perform his favourite party trick of getting his head under her legs and tossing her, which she thought was hilarious and retaliated with groans of joy, and a nose dive at him, barging in her turn.

'They both belong to me and are playing.'

'Don't lie,' he said, breathing heavily, his complexion that of an outraged beetroot. I wondered if he could be drunk but it was early in the morning; the conversation deteriorated to even more lunatic remarks on his part, parried by me with difficulty because he wasn't making much sense and he was so furious at my wickedness!

Luckily the dogs felt hot and tired and came to lie panting at my feet and with as much dignity as I could manage I leashed them both and left him declaiming to the empty sands, and took them to my car. I haven't been back to that beach since!

I don't like beaches with Chita either.

When we first achieved beautiful off-lead heeling, I did take her to one of our quieter beaches; very few visitors find it, but the locals know it. The road runs along the edges of the shore and in places you can park almost on the sands. At high tide in winter the sea can lap over the road. In summer it is lovely, and I can park, open the car and let the dogs lie in the fresh air, and watch the light change on the mountains opposite.

The sea washes the sand, murmuring gently; the oystercatchers cry; the shellduck court, and there is usually no one there but me. The dogs can wander as they choose; though they may never chase the birds.

The older ones at that stage would lie with the hatchback open, not bothering to run free, tired after their individual walks; Puma lying with her nose on her paws, seeing very little but aware I was near, Janus watching that puppy have her lessons.

We managed that for about six months without hazard.

One day Chita was walking by my side and the older dogs were both snoozing, this time, luckily, with the hatchback closed and the front windows open as it was a fairly brisk and windy day, the white caps on the waves blown towards us.

Another car drew up, braking noisily, a couple got out, opened the back of the car and out leaped a large dog that barked at Chita.

It was all she needed.

Off she flew at him, down the road, along the beach and out of sight. The other couple raced after them, whistling, shouting and screaming. I leaned against my car, knowing it was useless. A few minutes later my dog came back, pleased with herself. 'Saw him off, didn't I? Going to kill you, he was. Aren't I brave?'

'Pest,' I said and leashed her and gave her a lesson to remember; heeling and turning fast, making her really think. About half an hour later the other two owners appeared with their dog. They were both furious. No business to have a dog like mine loose; very dangerous. Was their dog bitten? No. I pointed out she had been under control and theirs had leaped out and barked at her, and they could have taken him out more gently and then it wouldn't have happened.

'We pay rates too,' they said, a remark which seemed to have no point at all till I thought hard about it and even then I wasn't sure.

I was consoling one of my club members with this story the other day. Her dog, which is not the same breed, is remarkably like Chita; lively, alert, eager, from working stock, and very fast to react. If she sees another dog she doesn't want to fight; she wants to play.

Other dogs however often can't distinguish between the two desires and don't respond. And other owners often mistake a play bark invitation for a 'get off I hate you' noise.

On this occasion, Jenny was on the beach with her dog and because Lou is liable to lunge out in fun and upset other dogs, she is kept, as Chita was, on a line, twenty-four yards long. She can run freely, have lots of exercise, but is safely under control.

Another family came on the beach with their dog and Lou did her famous rush out, I want to play act, and Jenny quite rightly checked her and called her in. Lou being as forthright and as energetic as Chita, came in fast, bouncing, and poor Jenny was shattered to hear the man of the family say, 'Just a minute. I want to watch that woman, she's vicious.'

I assured Jenny it was crass stupidity on his part, as he obviously did not have the least idea what type of dog Lou is. You have to check these dogs or they get into trouble and the checks aren't hard, but look it because of the speed with which the dog corrects itself. These dogs are much faster than we humans.

Like Chita, Lou is very quick to know the movements associated with a check and as you tighten your knuckles to jerk the lead, as Mrs Woodhouse recommends, the dog sees those knuckles and is in so fast that people think you have done something awful! In fact you haven't done anything; you started to correct and the little imp has read the signs before you have completed the action.

It can make it very hard to deal with a dog when it behaves like that.

Lou is only a year old and when she first came to club poor Jenny came in at a pace that shook even me, used as I am to people who take headlong dives with dogs that won't behave themselves. It reminded me vividly of my first club days with Janus who sorted me out in his own way, determined I would never get a swelled head because I could manage a dog.

I have since watched a number of people sorted out by Golden Retriever dogs who have a genius for making fools of their owners, and the more dignified the owner, the worse the dog seems to behave. I soon learned not to try and be on my dignity with Janus; it doesn't work!

Jenny had to work very hard on Lou but few people seeing them now would believe that the dog had been so difficult. It was only energy and puppy enthusiasm. Even now neither Lou nor Chita will sit still if someone tries to stroke them; and if Chita sees Edie and I don't let her go and have a 'word in Edie's ear' it is all I can do to control Chita at all. Edie is there and *must* take notice of her. We have tried having Edie ignore her. It doesn't work. One acknowledgement is enough these days.

Some days both of us still battle, not with a dog that is any way dangerous but with a dog that is going to do exactly as she pleases. Go and greet Edite; go and greet Bob; go and greet Digger; what Chita wants Chita still insists on having and as she can't have it, she is still having to learn and I am still having to sort her out, and at times I wonder why I ever bothered. There are easier ways to live. And wouldn't they bore me!

Then she hurls herself at my lap, licks my hair and ears, offers me her bone, her undying devotion, her paw, and moves away, to bounce back at me holding something I have dropped on the floor.

'You want it?' I always want it. 'Clever girl!'

Training Chita has involved teaching her to search and this is one exercise I wish all clubs would teach as it is so useful. It's so easy too, as the puppy search simply consists of having a favourite toy and throwing it into long grass, or hiding it in the house, behind cushions, under rugs, under books, or in boxes.

Pups adore hunting and this is a real hunt.

'Where is it, Chita? I want it.'

She bounces, like a fox pouncing on its prey. 'Got it, here it is, take it,' and she races at me, nearly banging into me but skidding to a stop as she can't learn to slow down; life is too exciting all the time, no time to waste: 'Must get on with it, never waste a minute, now what are we going to do next?'

She thrusts her nose at me.

'Take it, go on, take it and throw it again, and again and again and again.'

Chita's toy is part of the sleeve of one of my old jerseys stuffed with old rags; stitched to form a rectangle, about 8×4. It is soft to carry and she loves it. Sometimes she carries it thoughtfully out into the garden and sits with it in her mouth, looking at me.

'Come on, throw it.'

I do, and she rushes to find it, scratching at the grass, sending roots and stems flying, even though she could perfectly well pick it up without all that drama.

One of the favourite Trials search articles is a sparking-plug.

This is heavy and not easy to pick up and she digs at it with her paws and it flies backwards. That makes her cross so she 'weeds' busily round it with her mouth, which is funny, scrapes again with her paws and off it flies backwards.

'Goodness me, blow the thing, dear, dear!' her body says as she digs again.

In the end she does get it and comes over with it sticking out from between her teeth, looking as if she is smoking an odd-shaped cigarette. She dives at me again, sits in front and thrusts it at my hand, which can be painful if I don't watch her. I've not yet found out how to teach her an easy pick-up on this one.

Cartridge cases are easier to pick up. Half beer-mats are annoying as they often refuse to come off the ground; they need a paw against them to lift them but in long grass that isn't possible. I bend them – judges often don't.

One thing, she won't give up. 'Will pick it up, horrible thing, not going to beat me, pick it up if I have grass, nettles and thistles, too.'

She may pause, spit out a mouthful of grass and article and then gingerly pick it up in her teeth again and trot in.

On other days there is obviously a new scent in the air and she rushes round the garden scenting, nose up, asking what smell is on the wind. Then nothing will settle her down; she paces round and round, runs in, won't listen to me, and I have to abandon the idea and make her settle to something we can do on the lead so that she realizes she must do as I want. After all, if the house caught fire and she wouldn't come when called she would be in terrible trouble as she's much too heavy to carry.

Searching pays big dividends.

Janus was taught to search and I was once very glad I had taught him. We were to go to my mother-in-law's funeral. We stayed at a roadhouse, where the two dogs were allowed to sleep by our beds. Kenneth went a day early to settle the necessary business involved, and I came on with the dogs in my own car, arriving late in the afternoon after an absolutely hair-raising journey that ended in the rush-hour in heavy traffic. I am more used these days to country driving and not to towns and one-way systems and commuter traffic. This was Watford – not Wales.

I had travelled for about nine hours, with two breaks to walk the dogs, and I was very tired. I got our room key and then realized the dogs needed a walk. There was a big five-acre field behind the roadhouse and I took them in there, the key in my hand. A small yale key without a tag on it, but with the room number etched on the round part. The dogs, released to run free after a long day in the car, played and searched for rabbits and other interesting things and I watched them. I went with them to my room; and discovered I had dropped the key.

We had only been there half an hour. I couldn't face

confessing!

I put Puma in the car, took Janus back to the field, and rather forlornly said 'Seek.'

He began to quarter.

'Not there, you stupid dog. I didn't walk there.'

He barked.

There was the key. I *had* walked there. It had taken him about four minutes to find it, on a huge field, which I had wandered around rather aimlessly. I have never been so glad in my life that I had taught him to search, even though he can't do Trials as he is unable to jump because of his bad hip.

It paid off again years later with Chita.

I take my wedding-ring off every night, as my first wedding-ring had to be cut off when my knuckles swelled with arthritis. I now have a special place for it, but that night I just put it with my watch on my bedside table. During the night I reached out in the dark to get a handkerchief out of the cabinet drawer and must have knocked the ring on to the floor.

In the morning, no ring.

It was Sunday and we got up late.

We have a large goatskin rug between the beds. It is very shaggy. I crawled around the thing for an hour. No sign of the ring. But it had to be in the bedroom.

Chita had been trained to search.

But everything in the room must smell of me or Kenneth and how could she pick out what I wanted in a room I lived in, on a rug I walked over barefooted?

There was little chance, but if we vacuumed that rug the ring would be gone for ever and the ring had to be somewhere in the room.

I called Chita.

She isn't allowed upstairs so she came up suspiciously, apparently wondering if she was to be scolded and sent down again. One of my more peculiar lessons. Sensible to me and not to her. I watched her creeping and said, 'Don't be silly. I've lost it.'

Her ears pricked. She pranced after me, tail flying at full mast, waving eagerly.

I'd used her key phrase. The words switch her on.

I took her into the bedroom, pointed to the rug and said, 'I want it.'

I watched her nose go down, sniffing carefully, across the rug and back and then she stiffened, and pointed with her nose, and pawed the rug.

I didn't believe her. She had only been there twenty seconds and she didn't really know what I wanted.

There was the ring, by her paw, right at the bottom of the long shaggy furry tufts in the dead centre of the rug.

She danced in excitement and pelted downstairs and straight to the bread-bin.

Janus, not to be outdone, came too at a fast pace, and Puma who had been asleep and by now was quite blind, lifted her head, knew I was there, and I found her with her paws on the draining-board asking for bread, knowing for some reason Chita was about to be rewarded. They always picked up messages from one another.

Puma never learned to search or track. She was an air-scenter. She could scent a squirrel in a tree a hundred yards or more away; up went her head. When I tried to teach her to distinguish different scents she never made a mistake; she went to the right one instantly, but without looking at any others or nosing them. She would not ever get her nose on the ground. She would have been useful for mountain rescue as rescue dogs air-scent, and don't track; they need scent coming from crevasses and gullies and cracks; or blowing down from a ledge; tracking is useless if someone has fallen over a cliff.

So that if the mountain rescue people talk about searching and I talk about searching we are talking about two different things. I mean searching a small square for four objects which represent murder hunt clues, while they mean searching a mountainside for a victim of a climbing or walking accident, and saving a life. For a gundog, searching will be going through bracken or heavy cover to find a shot bird, which is different again.

We have to make it very plain to one another just what we do mean.

When I talk about agility, normally I mean a three-foot hurdle, a nine-foot long-jump and a six-foot scramble over an upright scale. But an agility competition involves tunnels, cat-walks, a seesaw, brushwood fences, hoops, and a variety of objects that aren't used in working trials. Working trials are nothing like field trials which are for gundogs; or sheepdog trials, or obedience competitions.

We may all use the same words for parts of the training but may well mean something entirely different.

If I ask my dog to fetch, she is to bring me in a dumbbell.

The sheepdog fetches live sheep.

The gundog fetches a dead rabbit.

I want Chita to find three or four objects hidden in a square of field; the square is fifteen yards square in the lowest stake and twenty-five yards square in the others. I may not enter the square; she has to do it alone.

The shepherd wants his dog to find the sheep which may be hidden from sight behind bushes or hummocks or walls, or in winter, buried under snow.

The gundog has to find whatever has been shot, has to mark it first and know where it is likely to be and may have to go after an injured bird or running animal; and be able to track it down.

The mountain rescue dog knows he has to find a person.

None of them could change places without a great deal of extra training.

Yet all of them are *trained* dogs; we have all trained our dogs, but though I can train a dog for living, for obedience and for working trials and for much of the guide dog and police work, I have never trained a dog for shooting or a mountain rescue dog. One can once one knows what is required, but the requirements are so different.

I don't expect Chita to go up in a helicopter or wear

a harness and be winched off a ledge. The mountain rescue dog must take that for granted.

I don't expect Chita to run out and disarm a man with a gun. The police dog must.

The shepherd doesn't expect his dog to search a square for things like sparking-plugs, washers, half beer-mats and cigarette boxes or half matchboxes or small pieces of material; but if we want our dogs to compete in Working Trials they must.

I don't expect my dog to lead me, when I am blindfold, to the shops or the station or the telephone kiosk or the bus-stop; but the guide dog must.

My dogs take for granted horses, cattle, sheep, goats. Town dogs often don't. A few weeks ago at the carnival, the regimental goat was there, with the Territorials, who were doing a demonstration after the dog club had put on their display. I was standing talking to one of the soldiers about the timing and where they were going to erect their mock machine-gun post which I thought might be in the middle of our arena, when Chita saw the big goat.

He was lying quietly chewing the cud, obviously well used to being part of army displays. I wasn't sure what she would do, but watched her, ready to prevent any silliness. She used to bark at any animals she hadn't met before.

She sniffed him. He turned his head and she quietly licked his nose. He went on chewing his cud. She dropped at my feet, to rest, not ten inches from him, as good as gold. People watching admired her, and I thought how it had all paid off; worth every minute of the time I have spent on her. 'Good girl.' She knew it and every inch of her coiled-spring body proclaimed that she was aware she was being very, very good indeed. Her eyes said so; her head said so; her posture said so.

'Good, aren't I?'

I stroked her nose, as we moved on, and she came up fast, trotting beside me, ready for the next experience.

She was fascinated as she watched the floats, decorated with flowers, the cage of 'lions' prancing round in their disguises; a cage of 'monkeys' all gibbering at the crowd; a lorry that was full of Dr Who characters; apparently hundreds of majorettes in their bright uniforms, marching in, with twirling maces, with tambourines, all sizes, all coloured uniforms.

A bevy of beauty queens, none of them older than twelve.

The fancy dress parade.

Soldiers in camouflage uniforms with guns.

The jazz band which Janus heard so that he leaped up from sleep and stared. 'I can hear that,' his expression said, excitement on his face.

People thrusting past us, children running, with candyfloss; other dogs running free, coming to nose our dogs; all our dogs collected together by now and the apparatus to be carried, with difficulty, dog leashed in one hand, heavy plank end in the other; down the field past a group of children doing a trampoline display.

Chita was entranced. So much to see; so many people, so much going on. This was the life.

We got the course ready, put the table out and she jumped on and posed there. Sitting as good as gold, queen of all she could see, with a grandstand view.

Her small face was so alive, her eyes brilliant, her look so eager, her body so vital that it is hard to think she too will one day age. I can't imagine Chita slow and steady, unwilling to sample everything that life has to offer her.

I rarely have to say 'Behave little bitch.'

It's much more likely to be 'You clever girl, aren't you clever,' and she looks up at me, glowing with excitement, her tail weaving from side to side, never stopping, as now she is secure in her world, that tail is rarely still; it tells me her feelings; it shows me whether she is settled on a track and it rewards me when I praise her.

She is sighing now.

'Come on, you've typed long enough; let's do some living.'

And as I stand up she will be up before me, leaping at the door, trying to open it. She is the only dog I know who can cope with the wrong side of a door if it is ajar; she tosses her head, and somehow uses her paw to flick it towards her, then gets her nose in it, and opens it with her teeth.

Life for me is as fascinating as it is for her as I never know what she will discover next; she does things I have never known other dogs do.

Above *Chita beside her favourite beach on the Menai Straits; opposite are the lower mountains of the Snowdon range.*

Below *Puma, Chita and Janus: sadly, Puma is only a memory now.*

Left *Janus and Chita staring hopefully at the bread bin. We want food!*

Below *The dogs in the room where they sleep beside the wood-burning stove.*

Right *Janus waiting for the call he never hears now.*

Below *This is a favourite part of his daily routine.*

Chita has to jump 9ft to qualify in working trials. We practise daily, mostly at 7ft. The jump is extended by a few inches a week as a Trial draws near, aiming to reach her peak just at the right time.

There is nothing so exciting to Chita as the search for her 'mouse'.
She has to learn to carry small things between her teeth
in case they get swallowed.

Left *I fit Chita's harness at the start of a track to indicate to her what she is to do.*

Right *Chita has found the article and this is how it has to be held up for the judges to see. She is now tracking on, searching for more.*

Her harness comes off immediately she has finished a track so she knows that she has completed the exercise. This is the reward for a good track: she adores jumping — and her 'mouse'.

Above *Chita is being set up for the 50-yd sendaway — straight away from me until I tell her to 'Down'. This is not an easy exercise to teach.*

Below *Chita waiting for something exciting to happen. Life is all excitment with her.*

Chapter Seven

I was walking through our nearby little town the other day when a voice said, 'Oh, it's *you*. I might have known.'

It was the owner of one of our club Golden Retrievers with her bitch; Heidi was pulling towards me, her tail beating. 'It's Joyce, I want to see her.' There was no way I could pass without a stroke for her and a laugh with her owner.

Long ago, talking to Puma's breeder, I asked her why she liked judging Breed dogs. It is not something I want to do. I could probably say truthfully that dogs are my passion; but not their show points, and not even the way they work.

The answer I got was 'Joyce, all those gorgeous dogs. And I can legitimately put my hands on every one of them; spend time with them, look at them in detail, get to know them. That's why.'

I get lost when I look at dogs.

I recently judged a little test between two clubs; judging is great fun and it is not earth-shaking. Although it is a responsible job, I don't want power; power over others is something that I feel ought to be outlawed.

There was I, with forty other dogs and forty people; and I had to work out which was best. They were all beginners, showing me how well they had trained their dogs.

A little King Charles Spaniel came on to the floor, his head up, his small body alive with excitement, his eyes watching his owner, his small tail whirling round like a propeller. He looked so funny it was very hard to concentrate on what I was supposed to be doing, because I just wanted to savour the moment, see dog and owner so happy together, just enjoying being out on the floor together, proving that they had done their homework.

A few minutes later a child came on to the floor with a Maltese Terrier, a white fluffy little dog, again full of happiness; child and dog presenting a very pretty picture, so that again I wished I weren't judging but could just watch.

I love watching the dogs.

My memories of Puma are of watching her run, free, on the field, the effortless thrust of her legs driving her over the ground in a movement that was pure pleasure to see, reminding me of the floating ease of a well-made racehorse; of the way a good show-jumper will balance itself and soar over the poles, a pleasure for the eye that can only be shared by those with the same passions.

My memories of Puma are of Puma greeting me, her ears flat, her eyes adoring, her hind legs slightly bent, 'sealing' towards me, and the joy on her face if I laughed at her and said, 'Aren't you a goose?'

I am not really very interested in breeding from my animals. I want to be with them, to show them the world and enter as far as I can into their world, trying to understand what it is on the grass that triggers excitement, trying to anticipate every movement, to interpret the sudden lift of a head and the seeking nose asking the wind what is there. Is it a rabbit, or stoat or weasel? Is it pheasant in the grass or the dark shadow of a hunting hawk?

There is nothing like being alone with my dogs on a windy beach, or in a shady wood; or over the fields. Is that a fox earth, there in the brambles? And that has to be an old badger sett. Is is still used? As we go towards it up come the dogs' heads again, sniffing, and at the entrance is new-dug earth and the mark of a big paw. Badgers. Yes. And still in residence.

There on the grass is the remains of a kill.

Hawk or fox or weasel?

Back I go to check in my books; to see if I have forgotten what I used to know, or confused the evidence.

Each of the dogs reacts differently. Each comes for a

walk alone; it takes more time but each dog must be individual for a time each day, alone with me, without the others, and not part of a pack. Even though humans do not recognize the pack, it is there, with more than two dogs. It does not take over, because you never allow it to do so, but leave them on their own, outside, hunting, and soon the rules you have tried to instil would be forgotten.

It is important that each dog recognizes me as the leader; that the youngster does not consider herself to be boss, as well she might in a natural state; that the others do not relate only to one another, and not to me.

So out we go, on the farm, down the lane, where in spring the bluebells flourish in a carpet that few see except for us; where I can find windflowers and primroses in all colours, because once this big estate was planted, and now it is wild, gone back to nature, with the garden flowers escaped and rioting among the wild flowers, with early purple orchids in spikes along the ditch and spotted orchids and tiny yellow flowers later in summer that no book of mine shows.

My garden bank now is wild with blue scabious, with ragged robin and with foxglove spires; they riot among the roses and are just as pretty, and I 'forget' to weed.

Out in the fields, the grass is bright with small flowers; and Janus comes first, these days on a tracking line because he is so deaf he doesn't even hear the clatter of the bowls being prepared at feeding time. He bumbles along the hedge, a clumsy dog, lumbering along, sometimes with little skips of excitement, sometimes with a sudden fierce lunge to catch a scent near the ditch, his head down all the time. He never looks up. Out he goes after Chita has been to play on the big field at home, and he follows every step she has made, faithfully. I have noted the line she took and the smells that interested her. The molehill where there was movement and her sudden swift eager digging; the patch of the grass which may have been the hedgehog, the interested sniffing into a clump of grass where the partridges may have been lying.

Janus goes over every inch that Chita walked, sniffs where she sniffed, cocks his leg where she puddled, ambles thoughtfully over every blade of grass, asking it to tell him its story.

Puma was very different. She had no interest at all in tracking where the other dogs had been. She came out of the doorway, and then, released, she floated effortlessly round the field, running for the joy of it, racing against nothing, against the wind, her eyes bright with the pleasure of living.

That done, and she would circle the field a number of times, before age claimed her, she would run to me and roll on her back and yearn at me. 'Love me, please love me,' and I would kneel beside her and she would push her head deep into my hands.

Later, when her brain was betraying her, that push into my hands was frequent; and then it became a desperate push against the side of the settee, against the floor, or even against the wall, and one day I realized that it was because her head hurt her.

So many memories of Puma, lying at my feet, stretching out her head against my shoe; Puma lying in the corner between the settee and the wall, her glorious colours even more glorious as if she had deliberately posed there against the white to show herself off, lifting her head to look at me, the light in her eyes there even when she was blind so that even our vet was not sure I was right. He knew it when she died. We looked down at her.

The light had gone from her eyes for ever and she had no eyes; only white opaque curtains that hid every scrap of the eyeball. She must have been unable even to see a glimmer of light and have lived in perpetual dark. No wonder she had needed me so much.

Puma, going up the field with me, close to me, my pockets containing two slip chains that jingled as I walked so that she could be off the lead and still hear me; though she obviously felt safer on her lead. If the other dogs went out too and ran off she could scent them, on the wind, and join them, but if the wind blew towards them she was lost and could come to me, her face bewildered.

'They've gone. Where are they?'

Janus would lumber down to look for her, nose her, and off they would go in a small game that seemed to keep him in contact with her. I was never sure whether he knew she couldn't see. Later I would take him in. Chita meanwhile played by herself, hiding a stick and finding it, racing round with a flower-pot bigger than her head in her mouth, playing the giddy goat (a role she now enjoys), butting at Janus, who would turn and tell her off. 'Go away. Playing with Puma. Busy.'

When I knew Puma was quite blind she and Janus went out without Miss Self Importance. She could be a nuisance, and far too rough with the older dogs.

Out on the field to play in the sun; Janus would leave Puma and hunt the hedgerows hopefully; you never know, there might be a rabbit. There never is; we have only ever seen two here, though I spent one breakfast-time, on a very wet day, watching a hare sitting in the river field, squeezing the water out of the fur of its ears with small determined paws, looking oddly like a girl setting her hair and combing it.

Out of the field to race, Janus never far enough ahead for Puma to lose; once she was leader, but now she was led.

Then in would go Janus, and Puma would come and hurdle. She adored the hurdle and would go over it endlessly, but one day she startled me as the wind had blown it down and I had, without realizing it, moved it about four feet to the left of its original position.

'Puma, over.'

And over she went, clearing the height faultlessly; in the old place, over a hurdle that wasn't even there.

I put it back. She was used to that spot. I didn't like seeing her vault nothing.

Out in the fields, Janus would ground scent, but Puma's head was up all the time. It was Puma who introduced me to the squirrel feuds and the squirrel-magpie wars. There were grey squirrels when we used to walk in Cheshire. I rarely see one here, and there are none on our land.

But there they were in the gardens and in the parks. Puma's head would go up, her nose would wrinkle and her eyes would try to seek out what was there and I would catch the quick flirt of a grey tail or see a bright-eyed head looking down at us. On one occasion Puma and I stopped to watch two squirrels over a hundred yards away on the ground. One had an acorn and the other hadn't and a fight began for the trophy.

'He's got my acorn!'

Both were tiny squirrels, perhaps litter mates from that year's nesting; and Puma appeared to find it as funny as I did. Such drama over such a small thing. There were other acorns in plenty a few yards away but that one was important to both.

On another occasion Puma's head went up and I looked above me to see a squirrel dashing along a branch for its life, pursued by two infuriated magpies. He had plainly been raiding their nests.

Nest-raiding was always a problem. My study then was upstairs, the tiny room over the hall that really wasn't big enough for a bedroom. Opposite were the nests in the gutters, made by many birds during the spring, and often the magpies would fly in and fly out again, a mouthful of tiny legs sticking out to show that they had been preying. Once a squirrel raced up the drainpipe and emptied the nest. The house was too far away for me to even shout and stop them. I could only watch helplessly, it happened so fast, as did the tiny death scene enacted on our lawn at breakfast long ago when my small daughter suddenly screamed.

We looked out to see the birds at the bird-table, and a magpie flying off with a thrush speared on his beak. He had come in, stabbed it and gone off again, fast. After that I took care to have the kind of feeder the bigger birds couldn't get at.

It was Puma who alerted me one day to another small drama.

We were driving through a village not far from

home; the church, with its Norman tower, was isolated from the houses by three fields on either side. The dogs were supposed to be lying down, but Puma liked to look out when she could see and watch the world go by. Everything fascinated her. Janus tends to sleep and only bark at other dogs if they come too near the car, but Puma took in everything we passed. She must have hated being unable to see.

I heard an odd noise from her, and looked at the pavement.

There was a mob of small birds, fascinated by something in the middle. I drew up and parked. The road was very wide and it was early morning and there was no traffic. There in the middle of the mob was a weasel, doing his death dance. He twisted and turned, he somersaulted and he span, a whirling animal, a mass of rusty fur, mesmerizing the birds that crept closer and closer, and closer. He poised himself and I knew that within moments he would spring and one of the unwary watchers would make a weasel's dinner.

I did the unforgivable thing and hooted. Watchers should never interfere, but it's a hard rule to keep at times.

The birds flew up and all that was left on the pavement was an enraged weasel, racing in circles, gibbering in fury at being baulked of his prey after all that work. He wouldn't go hungry long. He was quite unaware of us in our metal shell. Cars make good hides.

It reminded me of another occasion long before, when we only had Kym, our Siamese cat. We had left him in the caravan. We were up in the wilds of Scotland, and, driving in the Land Rover along the side of the loch, on a windy day when the waves were whipped to white, but sky and sea were a clear beautiful blue, we saw large birds fishing.

We stopped and watched three ospreys.

One of them caught a trout that must have weighed all of two pounds; a huge fish, that protruded from either side of his beak, fighting for its life, slapping him hard on each cheek. He stood, unable to cope, for some minutes, and we thought he was going to drop it back into the water. He was standing on a rock that reared its craggy head out of the sea.

The struggles became less, and he began systematically to hammer the fish's head on the rock, till it was quite dead, when he began to eat it. We watched the other ospreys pose as if to be photographed. We were far away from the known haunts of the birds and hope they still hunt the sea lochs, undisturbed, in a remote part of Scotland, where few people come and where we certainly would not have ventured without a Land Rover.

Puma often scented things that Janus missed, because Janus only air-scented bitch. My memories of Puma go back to a puppy running with her mother, racing to the wire of the kennel to nose my hand; walking her with her brothers Panther and Porky (whose proper name was Poirot) out in the fields and along the road, because Janus was once more lame and I needed exercise. He stayed in the shade of my car, in the kennel yard, after having had a gentle lollop round the fields where the foals galloped and the calves played and the dogs often ran with them, stretching out in a race against all the young stock. We could stand at the gate and watch endlessly and somehow, nine years ago, it seemed always to be sunny.

Porky was a dog that liked to talk.

He was beautiful and it was a tragedy when he died of the lead poison that affected all three of them. It was Porky's post-mortem that saved the lives of the other two. Panther died two years before Puma. His kidneys failed; the result of that long-ago accident. There was lead in the paint on the walls of a three-hundred-year-old barn; in the kennels where the three pups were put. Lead is sweet and the dogs get addicted to it; calves still die for the same reason. Long-ago paint can still cause problems and sometimes foreign paint may have lead in it too, which is why there is such a need to safeguard children's toys as children also will suck the sweet betraying flavour, and may die. Today I had a letter from Western Australia, about another four-month-old puppy that had been poisoned by lead paint, this year (1981). He too has survived. And today I read of the death of our club vice-president's young dog – a lovely up-and-coming future champion. Zorro died too of lead paint. It is still too much around.

Porky loved the world.

'Look! Duck!' he would exclaim, and if I didn't take any notice he would paw my leg and look up to make sure I had seen. Everything entranced him; ducks and geese; other dogs, and horses; all for his benefit in this wonderful big world he enjoyed for only five short months.

Memories of Puma go back to those days; to the two big pups lying in the dark kennel, unable to stand the light; to the endless days of worrying lest they too die, to listening to the hysterical squeals when an attack recurred; to me sitting with their breeder, who was helpless with a broken leg, waiting for the vet to come with the antidote while Panther screamed as Porky had screamed just before he died.

'Don't go to them whatever you do. Excitement triggers death.'

We closed the kennels and I sat and listened till someone came to take my place and later that evening I learned the vet had been and both pups had had the antidote. We waited.

We waited for weeks, and then with the skilled nursing both had from their breeder, and her husband and kennel staff, they began to recover. My father was dying then and Puma had to stay in the kennels. I couldn't travel with a young pup and I couldn't travel with a sick dog. When I was free I took her out.

I took her to town, and walked her round the shops and through the traffic. She was never afraid. She loved every minute, even after eleven weeks in the dark kennel, unable to stand the light, because lead affects their eyes.

Eight years later I was to look at her and think 'lead affects their eyes.'

She had large eyes for her breed; perhaps a fault but they were lovely eyes, and very expressive. The expressions on the dogs' faces on the cover of *Three's A Pack* are so typical. Puma, as always, enjoying herself immensely, laughing at the camera; Janus, bored by the whole procedure, wanting to go hunting on a trail all his own, lying there because he had been told to, so he was being a good boy; and behind is Chita, her imp face alert and eager, full of mischief, planning goodness knows what to do as soon as she is released to run.

Puma always moved so proudly, aware that she was beautiful, posing for the camera, posing for the judge, posing for me. She was immensely proud of her tail which was exceptional, the fur on the underside creamy white and very dense; and her 'petticoats' were dense too. Her face was light in colour, which gives a kinder expression than a dark face, to my mind. Chita has an impish face, where Puma was benign. The fashion now is for dark faces – goodness knows who decides. You can't show long-coated Alsatians either, which is a shame as they are lovely. They are, however, much cheaper to buy than show stock.

Memories of Puma include that long-ago day when she left her puppies, now ready for sale. She had gone back for her breeder to whelp as we expected complications and we got them. I left her, very reluctantly, because I hated being without her and because I wasn't going to visit her daily; that would upset her. I was to see the pups while Puma was taken for a walk; wearing her breeder's overalls and boots so that no scent of me was left and also no danger of infection as I was constantly in and out among other dogs and pups are very vulnerable.

I had been to Wales for a long weekend just before the pups were due. It was Bank Holiday. The family were boating and I intended to stay in our caravan and savour the peace. Only that year there was no peace as tents were in the next field and so were children from a deprived part of the country; though I enjoy other people, I did not enjoy children who seemed to think the side of my caravan was a latrine; and the hole where the tap was to turn off the water was used to shove mucky rubbish down. I complained to the site manager, left them to clean up the filth, and went home, leaving a note for the family.

I arrived home a day early and rang the kennels.

'I wish you had waited till later,' I was told.

Puma was in the middle of whelping and Puma was hating every minute and in considerable pain. Next day I learned she had a huge jammed puppy, right up under her ribs; the vet had come three times and finally had to pull it out by hand. She did not enjoy maternity and afterwards complications set in and she had to be spayed, after a long summer during which our vet tried everything he knew to save her for another litter. In the end she was operated on as an emergency one Sunday; her temperature was over one hundred and seven, and it took me ten weeks to get her back to even reasonable health.

When the puppies were weaned Puma came home.

I went to the kennels for her and she flew to my car and leaped in, not one moment of regret. Janus greeted her and they lay 'eating' one another, all the way home. I think he had believed she had gone for ever. He was overcome with delight.

I took them in.

I was eating my lunch when I saw them begin a game that was so funny that I forgot to eat.

Plainly, meeting again was pure heaven, and they wanted to recapture the moment of encounter; or that was all I could think.

Janus sat in the dining-room doorway, his face expectant and Puma went outside into the hall. She ran down the hall and hid in the kitchen. Janus sat on, ears pricked, eyes excited, waiting, and out Puma ran, and the two of them met and began to play, moaning with an excitement neither could contain.

Out Puma went again, this time to stay out of sight a little longer, while Janus, sitting again, edged on his tail nearer and nearer to the door. 'Oh, come *on*.' Back she bounced, and they put their paws round one another's necks and rolled over and over in a wild game which I didn't stop as they weren't doing any harm.

Each time Puma went out she stayed out longer, but the last time she came in Janus leaped at her in such excitement that one of his big canine teeth caught a large flap of skin on her head, pulling it loose. It was to start terrible trouble, as the flap needed to be seen by the vet, and Puma, always unable to leave an injury alone, scratched it septic.

She had to have a bucket on her head.

Puma's bucket collar was very funny. I walked into our local shop and asked the ironmonger's wife for a bucket. Plastic. 'What for?' 'For Puma.' The shop had other people in it, who stared, but the shopkeepers had a dog too and in no time at all the bottom was out of the bucket, eight holes were bored and it was strung on to Puma's collar.

Puma danced in temper.

I soothed her and laughed at her. 'You are funny. You are a *goose*.'

Oh, well if it was to make people laugh, that was different.

We had that wretched bucket on her for about six weeks. The injury had been well infected by her claws and was slow to heal. She had blue ointment round the outside and red ointment inside and needed only a white spot to be very patriotic.

The bucket came off in club when she worked and other dogs got used to Puma's funny collar. She looked as if she were wearing a poke bonnet. Janus wanted a bucket and would lie with his nose inside it if I put it on the floor. The wrong way round.

At one show the tannoy suddenly blared the number of my car. Would the owner please go to the secretary's tent at once.

I arrived to find an angry man telling me off for leaving my bitch alone as she had stuck her head in a bucket and couldn't get it off. I looked at him and explained it had taken some considerable time to make that particular bucket suitable for a dog to wear. I think he was about to report me to everybody under the sun, but fortunately realized he had made a fool of himself. After all how could she have got a bucket over her head like that? Few buckets are bottomless!

A few days later we went out to lunch with a friend who had two Jack Russells. Margery and I took all four dogs onto a disused airfield for exercise and they raced round in delight, as the place was totally deserted and we didn't have to worry about other people or dogs or cars.

One of the Jackies found half a tree, (at least it was compared with his size!) and he and Janus carried it for a long way. Puma found all kinds of smells and bolted in and out of bushes, every time giving the bucket, now rather dilapidated, another clobber that broke a piece off it. By the end of the walk it was in eight lumps, held on by string round her collar and she knew she looked funny. She danced for us, just out of reach, her eyes alight with laughter.

'Aren't I a goose? Aren't I funny.'

Memories are made up of this; not of shows and showing; not of the prizes and the rosettes and the days spent indoors when we might have been walking the hills.

Not of a dog in the ring among other dogs, but of my dog on her own, running against a background of trees, long shadows cast across the ground, thrown by the summer sun; of my dog leaping into the river, in a cloud of spray and coming out, and laughing up at me as she shakes the bright drops all over me; of my dog, lying at my feet, turning her head to look up at me, exchanging a look that nobody but us can share or interpret.

Of my dog, lying in my arms on that last day, unafraid. In her bed, where she was safe, leaving a world that had begun to frighten her and where laughter was forgotten. The last honour I could do for her, to give her death with dignity, before there was disaster – as there might have been, because who knows what dangers can threaten a dog that can see nothing and whose actions will be misinterpreted.

There are things one forgets. I was looking through my back copies of *Gamekeeper and Countryside* the other day when I came on a picture of Puma when she was two and underneath they have mentioned her, and the book in which she featured, adding 'On the front of Joyce's latest paperback her publishers have printed the following: "Joyce Stranger has two cats, two dogs and a PUMA!"' and I couldn't wait to see what they did with that!

In fact that piece caused relatively few problems; a number of children wrote to me in great excitement to know what I fed my puma on and what she looked like. They must have been very disappointed with her photograph.

Her pictures keep her in my memory for ever; a lovely bitch with a lovely nature, who I will never forget.

But life has to go on and I would never be without a dog. Each teaches us something. Puma taught me a great deal in her own way and in the end I learned how to live with a blind dog, taking great care to keep her environment secure. Janus is now almost eleven and his days are numbered; maybe not too soon, but none of us escapes in the end and death is something to be accepted, not feared.

Janus is teaching me how to live with a deaf dog.

Chita is teaching me all the time, she is totally unlike any other dog I have ever had: no two dogs can ever be alike. Dogs come to club, all so different, all with their own characters; and looking at them, I know that I am lucky, because my passion is not for prizes; it is for the dog itself and to learn all I can about its character, to help shape and mould it, to teach it to grow into the kind of dog other people look at and sigh over.

'I wish I had a dog like that.'

Anybody can, if you want to badly enough and take time and trouble to produce it, because of all creatures the dog is the one than can live closest to man, can be moulded by man and the RAF are right when they say that every owner gets the dog he deserves.

Careless people have careless dogs; nasty people have nasty dogs; angry people have terrified dogs; but those of us who care enough have the kind of dogs that give us pleasure all our lives, once we have shaped them to what we need. Pups have to be *trained*. And the dogs reward us, daily.

When Kym, my Siamese cat, died, I saw him running endlessly away from me through the woods he loved, where pheasants hid and birds scolded him and he could climb trees for ever.

Puma, night after night, came back to me in memory running by a summer brook, racing, not away from me, but towards me, calling to me with her eyes. Then she turned and jumped into the water and sent the bright sparks flying high.

I see her still, a young dog again, in her prime and the pride of her beauty, leaping effortlessly over the ground, in summer fields, by the water, and hope that somewhere she is enjoying the life she always loved, and she can see again.

Silly? Sentimental? Pathetic?

Is it?

None of us can know.

And if the end is silence and a long eternity, does it matter if while we are here we cherish a few foolish notions that harm nobody?

Sleep well, my beauty. Aren't you a goose?

Chapter Eight

My memories of Chita will always, I think, be of tracking. Janus didn't need to learn to track; he is a natural hunter as a retriever would be; hunting the hedgerows without knowing why, but he would naturally have thrown up birds for the gun; searching and quartering, zigzagging over the ground; still enjoying hunting for something I have hidden and still able to find it more quickly and easily than Chita who, though I have tried to teach her, does not do a patterned search. She does a fast, rather out-of-hand, scan of the ground, sometimes retracing her steps and going over the article she is looking for without scenting it, Janus never fails.

Tracking, to most people, is a mystery, but it isn't really, in one way. In another way it always will be mysterious as we have no idea what a dog smells or how his nose works. One of my favourite correspondents (when he has time, which is rarely) is a police sergeant in charge of police-dog training, who wrote me a long letter telling me what scent is made up of.

Scent of the ground we walk over, of crushed and bruised flowers and grasses.

Scent from our footwear. Scent from our occupation (builder, baker, candle-maker).

Scent from our bodies, every part of us smelling different; unseen fragments of skin and hair falling from us constantly.

The dog can follow all those scents and find a man after a long trail of several miles if he is highly trained, but he does have to be taught to concentrate for that length of time and young dogs need to be given experience.

It is easy enough to start the dog tracking. All you need is the dog's favourite toy, and either a fence to tie the dog to, or someone else to help you. You start with the dog tied up, and walk in a straight line for about ten yards, backwards, or shuffling along, turning constantly to shake the toy at the dog and say 'What's this then, do you want it?' in a very excited voice. You need to start on heavy vegetation; a field with plenty of good thick grass is best.

Also it is easier when first teaching to go in a straight line; it is much easier to help the dog if you know exactly where you have walked, so that the first tracks can end up at a post or a pole or a rail in the fence; or walk towards a tree. You have to take care that the dog doesn't think it can only track to one post, as it may associate something you did not mean it to associate with tracking, like always going towards a tree or a telegraph-pole, or along the line of a hedge or a fence, or through a gap in the hedge.

Chita's first lessons were given us by police-dog handlers, who always knew just how to get her very excited; a small puppy tugging on her lead, being allowed for once to give tongue loudly. Making a noise is after all part of many dogs, as anyone who has ever heard a pack of hounds knows. Many modern German Shepherds are remarkably noisy. Puma rarely made any sound except her warning bark.

We were once in the park when a very small man with a very red face and a very large Basset Hound came pelting past, totally out of control. The Basset Hound was making enough noise for a whole pack of hounds. The dog's nose was down, he was tracking dementedly and he was yelling at the top of a very loud voice.

'On a fox track,' his owner panted as they rushed past us and disappeared fast into the distance, still sounding like a whole hunt. I hoped he wouldn't have a heart attack.

A moment later Janus and Puma caught the scent and gave me problems but I tackled them differently. Those around me were probably considerably intrigued by our progress towards the car park. Step, SIT. Step, SIT. Step, SIT. It was the only way I could keep my two from charging off at top speed as they too had caught the scent of fox.

A year or so later I was walking with our future
daughter-in-law who at that time was a warden of a
nature reserve that was being developed in an old
sand workings. The sand quarry was now a lake, a
very dangerous lake with quicksands so that a major
part of her duties was to stop small boys swimming
there; there was an island in the middle; the old
sandhills had been planted and were rapidly being
covered by lush vegetation and many varieties of bird
had moved onto the lake, among them Canada geese.
There were foxes, and her son one day found a dead
fox cub lying in the layby near the house. He is now
our step-grandson; it is rather nice to acquire a ready-
made family, as babies have to grow up before you can
do things with them. We have four grown-up step-
grandchildren, as well as the five under-fives, who
belong to our two sons.

Older children can be pressganged into helping with
all kinds of things. I borrowed our step-granddaughter
and her friend a few weeks ago to help us with a
display of dog agility at a carnival. We had dogs to hold
and hurdles to carry and a tunnel and catwalk and a
table; Cathy and Corinne were extremely useful.

But at that time our son and Vivienne were engaged
and not married, and she was still working at her job
in the reserve. It was a very peaceful place till the
geese came in and started calling, which happened
most evenings. There were duck as well, and a variety
of wild animals.

One bright summer afternoon we walked around
the lake, Janus and Puma leashed, because of the birds;
neither was reliable if it came to chasing; Janus can
never resist balls either; he will stay for hours while
balls are thrown round him, but if he is running free
and a ball crosses his path he fields it automatically
and runs off with it. So leads had to be used.

The place was not easy to walk on as the paths are
sandy and it had been a dry summer and the sand was
soft, filling our shoes. We came to a sloping dune and

began to walk down it. Halfway down both dogs lunged towards the bush beside the track, simultaneously, and I finished up skidding on my seat down into the dune bottom, hanging onto them, and being exceedingly annoyed with both dogs. Viv laughed; I must have looked extremely funny and after a moment of outrage due mainly to pain, I joined in.

We walked round the lake and met the gamekeeper.

'You have the most unobservant dogs I've ever seen,' he said.

'Unobservant?'

'There was a dogfox basking in the sun the other side of that bush as you went by. He went off in the opposite direction just as you and the dogs came to this side of it. How come your dogs can't even smell a fox?'

'They did,' I said and told him of my undignified slide down the dune, both dogs pulling like mad to get to the other side of the bush. He joined in our laughter.

On another night a fox got one of the Canada geese on the island. The poor bird was a long time dying. We later found the part-eaten body half-buried not far from the scene of my rapid descent down the sandslide.

Often there were scrapes either made by cubs or by adults trying to bury their food and making false attempts; we were never sure. They were certainly made by foxes. The paw-prints were plain to see, and it was nothing unusual there to see a fox lope off, turn and stare you out, one paw raised, eyes bold, and then slope off into the bracken, often with a rabbit in his jaws.

It was there I first learned more about tracking because there was always something for Janus to track; often we had no idea what, but he would keep his nose down on a trail till we pulled up short at wire fences.

With Chita, tracking was to be part of her competition life. Also, with her type of brain, she needs to be occupied. She came with me today for the post and papers and carried the newspaper down for me. Janus carries it too, taking his turn, holding it in his mouth, stepping out with a regal air; Puma would never carry anything except food. She often took her slice of brown bread to eat in her bed, probably because she felt safer there than anywhere else and knew the other dogs would never come near her in bed; that was her den; her sanctuary. The others ate in the kitchen. They still do, neither of them showing any need to take food away lest the other grab it. It is one thing neither would dream of doing, though if Janus drops his and can't find it fast enough and is nowhere near, Chita eats it quickly and then stands, looking innocent. He looks puzzled. 'Where's it gone? I haven't eaten it,' his face seems to say. 'Can't think how that happened, can you? We both need another piece. That's gone.'

Janus realizes then what has happened and wails and has to have another piece. Then Chita feels frustrated, sure he really had two all the time and she only had one after all; the other didn't count. So she asks for more; it's time to be firm. No more!

Chita learned about tracking. Her head went down and she began to search the ground for telltales. She learned fast, working out the trail, finding her toy and having a game as a reward.

I learned how to lay a track that was longer than a few yards.

Track-laying is a skill; you have to watch what you are doing and how you do it. With a young dog you double-track, going out and coming back along the same path. It is vital to know where that path is, for if the dog goes wrong you are lost and have no idea how to help it find the track again. You must also know the wind direction as scent blows around and two tracks close to one another could confuse the dog.

So, to track-lay, when teaching the dog, I go out with poles, to mark the track, and with a clipboard on which is a sheet of paper on which I can mark any landmarks, or with a hard-backed notebook as an hour later you may forget just where you made a turn.

You need two markers: so line up on a branch sticking out of the hedge with a telegraph-pole behind it or a chimney in line with a church steeple, or a corner of a barn with a large white post behind it. So long as both stay in line you know you are straight.

A lot of people have problems in walking straight, me included.

'Remind me to teach you to walk in a straight line,' Edie said the other day, as I didn't; I was watching Chita and not where I was going, which is a hazard of training a dog.

We weren't tracking; we were practising a complicated piece of heelwork.

The track is laid by walking out on it; at first when the dog is inexperienced, you walk with shuffling steps and come back again to the start over the same line. Later it is only necessary to walk one way, and then to make sure you don't cross the track anywhere or walk near it, as wind can blow scent around and scent can travel a fair distance; the path you took going out could be confused with the track you laid on purpose.

You also discover very fast that it's necessary to plan where you are walking in a field or you end up in the middle without any way of getting out again without crossing the path you have laid and you have to abandon that track; and tracking fields aren't easy to come by even in the country. You can't track in a hayfield, a cowfield, or a sheep field; you can't track where crops are being grown and the farmer may have just put fertiliser on the ground. It is necessary to ask permission, to ask questions as the farmer doesn't always know what you want.

I have the use of several fields on one farm, where I trained their young dog five years ago, when the farmer, who is not a young woman, was on crutches, waiting for a new hip joint.

Even so, I have to make sure that nobody is going to walk there.

One day when we were beginning to do rather well,

I laid a track and took Chita for a walk as I wanted to wait for twenty minutes before she worked it. I took her back, went into the field to start and saw a happy birdwatcher, using field-glasses, wandering all over our carefully-laid track.

He looked at me and asked if the poles were mine.

I explained what they were for.

'Sorry, I'll go,' he said. I don't think even now he realizes why it wasn't possible for her to track; he had walked all over the ground I had carefully laid the track on and his wellington-boot marks were everywhere. You can't see tracks – they are only footsteps.

He went home and I let Chita run free and was entertained to see her track off my line, very seriously, following where he had gone. As he had been walking entirely aimlessly it was a most remarkable sight, as she bumbled round from bootmark to bootmark, going nowhere fast in circles.

Chita is very solemn when she tracks. It is what she was born for. I have immense problems with her and her harness. Tracking harnesses go round the dog's shoulders, with a second piece round the body, and a strap underneath. They are, if taken apart, like a Chinese puzzle as you try to fit them together and I hate having to clean it. They need frequent cleaning with good saddle-soap to keep them supple and comfortable and of course have to be cleaned up if they get wet as they are extremely expensive (around £20 for a good one) and the leather will dry out and crack.

She sees her harness and tries to leap into it; squealing in excitement. She gets her head in the wrong part and we have a tussle to get it right.

'Going to track; going to track; going to track.'

She can't believe it. *Really* going to TRACK. It isn't something we do every day. It has to be a treat; who wants to eat an icecream daily, or strawberries, or even have the same favourite meal day after day, without a break? Dogs are no different. Train them too much and it's all a bore. Train them just enough and it's wild delight. A real treat, that lovely thing we do together.

I over-trained Janus, because a lot of people now train collies and you can keep them at work, and I didn't know then about different breeds needing different kinds of training; you can't keep gundogs at work in the same way. I find with this little German Shepherd that she too soon tires of a routine; it needs to be varied, so we never do the same thing twice running, though we always do the same exercise in the same way.

She learns too fast and does things before she is told which loses points and can get her in to trouble, just as a showjumping horse that tries to take a jump before it is in the right position can get itself into trouble, and fail through being too far away or too close, and by not paying attention. Training is to teach attention all the time.

Dog and horse training are very similar, and few people do either slowly enough. Take the dog too fast and you may find it can't absorb what you are trying to teach it. I found tracking with Chita so exciting I did probably take her too fast; and that lack of experience showed when we had problems in competition tracks.

So we are having a rest and starting again and going to make very sure that now she is mature she *isn't* hurried. Enough to keep it fun; enough to do it at the speed she can manage. I was spoiled by Janus who has years of experience of his own behind him and who understands what he is doing; Chita doesn't yet.

If she loses the track she doesn't search sensibly as Janus does, knowing it can't be far away. She casts in vast circles, pacing fast, air-scenting. 'It's gone, it's gone, where is it, can't find it, what's happened?'

At this point too the handler is often in trouble on an unknown track as you don't know what has happened. A fox might have tracked across, or a rat or a stoat or a weasel; or another dog may have come from somewhere and gone off again; a flock of birds might have landed and fouled the whole area. There might have been a horse and rider through the field. That did happen once; I found horse-shoe marks in three places on our track. Now I sit and watch the field. No one is supposed to use it but me. People trespass.

Someone may have come into the field and stood there, shooting; telltale cartridge cases usually betray that. Nothing to do but collect the used cases and pocket them for searches and give up for the day, as there is rarely another field near by which you can use.

If the dog can do the track, it is like the realization of a dream. There she is, intent on the ground, her nose down, as she breathes in, taking deep sniffs. 'Is this alright?' Another step, and another; and she has to come up for air and pause and think, and breathe deeply and then down goes her head, and her whole body attitude tells you she is concentrating intently, smelling something you can never smell, getting information from the ground that you can never get. You can see where the grass is broken, where a twig has snapped, where there are telltale footprints in the dew; but when the ground is hard and there is no sign on the turf, *you* are lost.

Did I walk there? Surely not, but you line up again on the markers and yes, she is right after all. There is the cartridge case you dropped; she noses it and stands, and looks at you. 'Want it?'

Some dogs pick it up, but not Chita, not yet. She is too eager to know where the track goes, where the track ends, where you have been walking. 'What did you stop there for?' her body asks, pausing where you paused, because the ground was unusually bumpy and you thought it better to re-line on something else and take a corner.

The corner is marked hard with a telltale shuffle as she isn't yet used to turns. She runs over it, loses the trail and does her fast little anxiety dance.

'Where's it gone, can't find it, where's it gone?'

Being Chita, she is intensely anxious; no mild anxiety for her. Drama every time. I reel her back and soothe her. 'Clever girl, seeeek, seeeek, seeeek.'

She remembers, her nose goes down and she finds the trail again. Her body shows her relief and interest. 'Oh there it is, wonder what's at the end of it?'

Off she pelts and I have to slow her, or I will be flat on my face.

'My mouse!' She seizes it and does a little war-dance, impatient for her game, too impatient to wait for the harness to come off. The harness goes on at the start of every track and not before; a trigger to set her mind working. 'I know what that's for; I know why that's on me,' her attitude tells me. She never lets me harness her quietly; she gets her leg in the wrong place, her head in the leg-hole, leaping to get it on, 'quick, quick, quick.'

It is the same when it comes off, as she is already pulling herself out of it even before the buckle is unlatched.

One day, I hope, she will wear our good-luck harness.

It is over fifty years old, patched and worn and loved; it has belonged to two champions; to two men who made their dogs up to the highest degree possible. To Dan Hare, who gave it long ago to John Cree, who used it for his Working Trials Champion, Quest of Ardfern. It was then sent to me for luck when it was no longer up to everyday use. But maybe, one day, in the far future, when a dream perhaps comes true, I will put it on her for a track that will make her, not a champion because I don't think either of us is up to that, but winner of the top award that we want, so that one day I can write after her name the magic letters CD.Ex, UD.Ex, WD.Ex, TD.Ex. We may never do any of it; if not, so what? It's fun trying. Once it stops being fun the dog is under pressure and then it's time to review your priorities.

Meanwhile it is necessary always to remember what Edie said when I first began with her.

Success only comes before toil in dictionaries.

And also, if we fail, it won't be the end of the world – it's a hobby, not a life's goal.

*   *   *

For those of us who enjoy being with a dog, tracking gives something that other people can't understand. Out there, alone on the hills or on the moors, or near the sea. Nobody but you and your dog. We are so lucky, living where the high hills rear to the sky, where the kestrel hovers overhead, and where, when I was walking Janus only two days ago, pheasant chicks were hiding in the long grass and ran as we approached. He was leashed and I stood and watched the frantic scurry, the mother fussing, the babies flying on their legs, their wings not yet grown enough to take to the air.

The long grass shook as they fled.

A moment later a kestrel was above us; and then I was under the trees, looking for the field where I thought I might lay a track for Chita. But the field was full today, and black and white Friesian calves, half-grown, tossed their heads and heels at us and fled at the sight of the dog.

Early in the morning we can track on the dunes, but later in the day the visitors come and there is no land that has not been walked over, or will not be. Nowhere to lay a track. Soon she will not need much unused ground and I often now lay her track where geese or sheep have been grazing.

In the winter I can walk in the hayfields, but not now.

They will soon be cut. Later we can try the hardest tracking of all, when the wheat and barley has been reaped and gathered in and we may venture on the stubble fields.

Stubble is hard on both of us; hard on the dog's paws. There is no way we can practice except by doing it and sometimes Trials tracks are on stubble. After all, this is pretend police work and the man running from justice is not going to be careful where he runs.

Stubble-fields have three directions: across the grain, in a straight line, down the cut line, and across the furrows diagonally. All of it has to be learned by the dog, because there are different scents. Walk on earth and there is one scent; walk on bruised stems and bruised weeds and there is another, and then go in another direction and you may get either scent.

Some people can track from field to field, learning to track in barley, then wheat, then rye, but few farmers like people walking in their crops and though we had one search in a wheatfield, the farmers here would not like it at all if we ventured into standing grain. Because of this many of us have to take our dogs on to ground they have never experienced before and the result is predictable.

We have not tracked in wheat, but recently we had to search in wheat. The wheat was high, well above Chita's head and Chita can't bear me out of her sight.

I sent her into what was meant to be a square; but a square in wheat, though marked out with posts, is remarkably hard for both handler and dog to see. Somewhere in that overgrown space were three tiny objects, not more than three inches square, in an area twenty-five yards square. And I can't go into the square to help her.

Chita went into it forlornly when I sent her and came straight out and looked at me.

'Can't find anything in there. You're daft,' she seemed to be saying. I don't like putting words into a dog's mouth, but this little bitch is remarkably expressive.

I rather agreed, but you don't tell judges you think the set-up is daft!

'Chita, I want it.'

She ran in, and found herself in the middle of nowhere, lost, and leaped, a high desperate kangaroo leap. 'Oh, you haven't gone.' I could see the stems shaking as she ran and knew from the pattern that she wasn't searching; she was having a very major Chita worry.

Should I bring her out? We were almost certainly doomed to failure.

It hadn't been a good day as the judges had decided we would work in catalogue order and my real name begins with a letter even further down the alphabet than S and Chita does her best early in the day. So do I!

It was late on; we had spent the morning wandering

forlornly in the rain; had had a few chats with other luckier people with names beginning with letters high up in the alphabet, were working, or waiting to work, or had worked. We played with her quoit. We had another walk and a coffee, and lunch, and another coffee, and conversation, and went to see if they were anywhere near us and they weren't. The day seemed endless.

It was four o'clock before we did anything and we had arrived at nine after a three-hour journey, which seems absurd. I wished we could have come after lunch.

Why on earth did I even *want* to compete, I wondered, as I sat in the car and wished it wasn't a day when there seemed to be little on the radio but religious programmes.

Now we were actually working.

Working?

'Help,' said Chita's body as she leaped high again and shot up on two legs to see where I had gone.

She came out, looked at me and did what she often does when she is desperately worried. She spent a penny. Sheer panic. She didn't need to; we had already seen to all that.

I knew that was all my spare marks gone and that the judge would comment. I was right.

'Chita, I want it. There's something in there; go and find it.'

Time was running out. We only had four minutes and nearly three had gone. In she went. Wild leaps towards the sky and that desperately anxious little dark fox-face again. Then she vanished and she really was hunting and just when I had given up hope, she found one object and arrived with it in her mouth. 'Here you are, aren't I *good*?' It was a square of thin leather.

I praised her with delight; we had at least one quarter of our marks, we needed three-quarters to do any good and whatever we did now we wouldn't make up to the required total, but she had ended successfully in a totally new situation that she had hated. And that alone was worthwhile.

Tracking can bring adventures; some of them, in the country, adventures you could do without. Parks and town moors don't bring quite such hazards.

Last year I decided to have a change from dogging and go riding in my spare time, when I could find spare time which is never easy as my life is pretty full; I often have to get up extra early to make time to write.

The stables are in an isolated place and they own a number of fields. They have bantam cocks in plenty; too many for the few hens, but the eggs always seem to hatch out cockerels and though some are sold there isn't the demand for them that there might be. So life is fraught as little fierce cocks swoop on one another, oblivious to the humans and horses in their way and fight.

They may fight at the edge of the riding paddock so it is as well that the horses are used to them since some of the riders are not.

I had my ride and was telling my instructress, as we walked back towards the stable, about our tracking. She had never seen a dog track and asked if I would like to show her what Chita did. I could lay the track in the big field on the far side of the house. No horses had been in it for a fortnight; it was being rested.

I laid the track, but in the end worked it alone as our watcher was called to the telephone.

We were to work in a sloping field, with outcrops of rock well covered by thorny bushes. There was a good straight stretch from the top of one hummock that I could reach by a detour, and I could bring the track back to the stile, and go out without crossing my own path in any way.

I went round the back of the field, put my starting-pole in at the top of the hummock and, using a telegraph-pole lined up on the house chimney, tracked down towards the car which was parked some hundred yards from the field. I put one small plastic lid on the track and ended with 'mouse', who is made of blue denim by the ex-police inspector who used to train the Metropolitan police dogs. The dogs love Roy's mice.

Midway on the track was a bush, and in it I heard a rustle, but thought little of it. Probably a bird turning over leaves looking for insects.

Chita had been lying in the car watching me ride; she had been barked at by several small Dachshunds and a Labrador. Puma was lying by Janus, her nose on her paws, aware of us but unable to see. I stroked her and gave her a titbit and she licked my hand; Janus sat up, eyes bright. 'Puma having titbits, where's mine?'

I gave him his. The back of the car was open and the dogs were fastened to the car by their leads, just in case the bevy of house dogs came back or Janus was tempted to chase a bantam cock, strayed into the car park.

Somewhere behind us a guinea-fowl suddenly screamed and Puma barked and I calmed her. A ride was coming down the lane; the horses that hadn't been out were calling to those that had and the bantams were joining in.

I wondered, as I took Chita out, who could think the country was quiet.

I stayed by the car as the file of horses went past, holding Puma's collar and talking to her so that she didn't bark and startle them. Her head was up, sniffing. She had grown up with horses and it was a smell she knew well. She relaxed and so did Janus. 'Horses gone. Didn't touch car. Don't need to bother.'

I took Chita round the field, up to the hummock and put on her harness. She now would sit at my side while farm animals and horses passed and I did not have to do more than command her. She watched, ears pricked, eyes bright, as if she were at a parade or a pageant; all the world puts on its finery just for Chita.

She hadn't had a track for a couple of weeks as it was high summer and everywhere was under crops, lambs, or hay. She danced dementedly, making me curse her, as I struggled to get the harness on properly and she struggled to get into it any way at all and we began with it on both backwards and inside out.

I scolded her and began again.

This time the clip for the longline appeared to have vanished and proved again to be on the inside. We began again and this time I did get it all correct, fastened the longline, released her, and was just able to take up the strain and stop myself pitching fast down the hummock and on to the rocks as she got the scent at once and flew off.

Down the track with me hanging on, remembering the judge who said, 'Hasn't anyone told you not to run with your dog?' I nearly handed him my dog and said 'Show me,' remembering the judge who said, 'I've never seen a problem like yours,' and went on to tell everyone of the remarkable day when his wife had tried to show me where I was going wrong with Chita's 'stays' and given up in dismay. His letter starts my last chapter.

'I've never seen a dog like yours.'

That seemed to be the story of my life with Chita. I hadn't, either, but it's all due to her overpowering desire to do everything she can pack into her life; do it fast and do it before she is told and get there first. If she were a horse and show-jumping we'd be round that course so fast no one would be able to see us, though we might well have everything down and splendidly down as we careered full tilt. If she were a racehorse she'd be front runner. If she were human she'd be a menace!

Now she had her nose down and was going more slowly and I gave a sigh of relief and was thankful I was wearing gloves. When we started she tracked much more carefully but when she had a hot scent she went at speed. This was fairly fresh; I had only laid it ten minutes before I took her on to it, as we had to get home – and here everywhere we can track seems to be at least twelve miles from home.

It was good ground with thick grass, lots of clover, which must make a good strong smell when walked over, interspersed with thyme, again smelling strongly, even to a human nose.

Down towards the brush and Chita heard that rustle, made a quick detour and charged the bush.

It was a big mistake.

Out came four goslings and an infuriated goose, her head down, her wings spread, to find a dog, a longline and a human by her nest, and for one brief second she didn't know who to chase.

Luckily for us she decided to chivvy her babies back into the nest before she came out to deal with intruders; making a great outcry about it, she sent them scurrying. Then she came at us fast, wings spread, bawling.

We hadn't waited; Chita had given one appalled look at what she had roused and she was hurtling towards the car; I did the only thing possible and dropped her line, which wouldn't snag when she went under the fence as it was only post-and-rail designed to keep horses in.

On the other side of the car park two riders having lessons had stopped to look, while their instructress watched too, as Chita made the car with me only a short length behind and the goose now in hot pursuit. Luckily the back was still open.

I slammed down the hatchback.

Unharness her later.

I got into the driver's seat and slammed the door.

The goose, baffled, went back to her babies.

It was some days before either Chita or I tracked without a feeling of considerable wariness. I avoided fields with bushes in and looked hard at the hedges, but since then we have never been startled by anything worse than someone shooting in a field nearby, or the sudden wing-clap of a startled pigeon in a tree above our heads.

We have only done two competition tracks. Neither was a success.

The first was on a very hot August day on a stubble-field; we were due to track at eleven but both competitors before us were late so we tracked at noon, with the sun blazing down and me too hot, in shirt sleeves, an event that rarely happens as I can soak up any amount of sun and it's rarely too hot for me; in fact it's seldom warm enough and I seem to spend the summer in jerseys.

The track went uphill; the stubble was sparse and the soil was dry dust. The headland, not very far away from us, was dense grass and people had walked over it; Chita knew it and apparently unable to find any scent on the dusty ground, walked over by someone half an hour before, was determined to go to the headland where others had walked only minutes before, even though it was some distance from her track. There was a strong wind blowing from the headland to us. It was obviously full of scent to her.

No way was she going to do her track. She was hunting the air for scent.

We ran out of time; afterwards I took her far away to a little paddock and laid her a track of my own and let her run it, so that she did not lose her confidence or for that matter, so that I didn't lose mine. She did it perfectly and was rewarded and her last memory of that day would be of success and not of failure. Most dogs failed.

Her search was no better.

Yet early on that day she had done a search in the lowest stake and got full marks. I decided a lot depended on the amount of wind, of sun and on the articles the judge had chosen as some are distinctly unpleasant to some dogs, and also on the time of day.

Her second track was also a disaster.

That day was a winter day, and we were to track high on the moors. I left home the evening before to stay with Joy. She has students to live with her in term-time but this was Easter and there were just the two of us. She was to look after Janus for me so that for once I could have just the one dog. Puma had died three weeks before. It was our first visit without her and Joy missed her too when I took only two dogs out of the car.

Both dogs knew Joy's home well and had been

sitting alert and eager long before we reached the door. They had pricked up their ears as I turned into the lane that led to her road.

Out to greet her two Shelties, out to see that nothing had changed in the garden and then in to circle the house and make sure nothing was different there. We spent an evening talking over old times, having known one another for nearly nine years, with plenty to remember as both of us worked our dogs. Joy far more successfully than I. She had sometimes been my passenger, and as well as shows to remember there were journeys to remember; days when we couldn't find the venue; days when we were held up by traffic, or days when we drove through torrential rain and wondered why we bothered to go on; or days when it was such lovely sunshine and we passed such beautiful places we were tempted to stop and forget all about the show.

Somehow, we never did.

This time I had an added hazard. I was to report to a farmhouse in the middle of nowhere on the Yorkshire moors at 7.15 a.m.

'You *what*?' said Joy. 'Obedience was never like this!'

I showed her the letter. I was to track at 8.00 a.m.

Which meant that I had to get up at four-thirty and be away by five if I were to make it; and it would be dark, and might be snowing and I had never driven that way before. Janus was to be put in Joy's bedroom with her two dogs when I left, to prevent him howling. He hates being left behind.

I poured over the map and planned my route meticulously, knowing that trouble would come in the last two miles as I couldn't find the road that led to the farm on my map.

And we hadn't one that showed more detail.

My alarm clock went at four-fifteen.

I got up sleepily. There wasn't such a time. I wanted toast and coffee first. I crept downstairs and let the dogs in the garden. I crept back up and put Janus and his vet bed, and a biscuit for him and one each for Joy's two dogs, who were awake, down on the floor, and closed the door softly. Joy never even moved, unaware of the three busy dogs eating and greeting one another before settling down to rest.

'And the best of British luck to *you*,' Janus's expression said. He had no desire to join us, getting up in the middle of the night, and seemed happy for once not to be coming too.

Chita, of course, fussed all through my hasty breakfast.

'Where are we going? You taking me? What are we going to do?'

I prepared for my day.

Rain gear. An extra jersey; a warm hat; gloves, spare clothes as it looked like being very wet. Wellingtons and a change of socks and shoes. My lunch; which as it turned out was inadequate for Arctic temperatures and a lot of running around. A flask of coffee for me; water and bowl for Chita and a small meal for her after she had worked; she watched with interest, rushing round with me, refusing to settle, occasionally squeaking in excitement and having to be hushed; it was easier to let her come with me as I loaded them up, then to leave her squealing to me to hurry (neighbours would have loved that) or leave her in the house where she would also have squealed.

I gave her her dumbbell to carry out to the car, and I found the show directions; her tracking harness and line; and 'quiet for goodness sake, dog, it's the middle of the night,' not even street lamps alight, and dark as the inside of an elephant.

'And we are not at home where no one can hear, but in a suburb, a street of houses, where people lead more normal lives than you and I, little dog.'

At last the car was loaded, but I was going out of the back door as the front needs a hefty slam and I didn't want to leave Joy in an unlocked house. I wrote a hasty note on an envelope I stole from her bureau, feeling like a sneak-thief, as I had to open two drawers before I could find a pen; I labelled the envelope 'back door key' and locked the back door from outside and posted the key into the hall.

It felt a remarkably silly exercise.

Suppose she didn't see the envelope?

It was the first thing she did see when she got up. She had been wondering if I had left her unprotected by an unlocked door, and felt mildly worried but couldn't be bothered to get up at such an unearthly hour to see, and she had three dogs in her room!

Meanwhile Chita and I took off into the dark; through the short cuts, nobody else around, not even a milkman, and on to the motorway, where we had the world to ourselves. It was cold outside and frosty, and it was very dark, and our headlights cut swathes through the darkness. On we went and came to Huddersfield, which was lying quiet, a maze of one-way systems. It's a good job it was deserted as I could take them slowly and it didn't matter if I was in the wrong lane as I am, invariably. It's a very confusing town. I go on to places I never intended to go to, to avoid causing trouble by changing lanes.

Out again on the minor roads and into nowhere.

We climbed, and the moors stretched bleak and dismal.

On again, past villages with names that sound strange after our Welsh names and I realized suddenly that I am now used to Welsh and not to English. 'What strange place names English villages have,' says our post mistress, looking at an address on one envelope. Weeping Cross. I hadn't thought about it before. Llandudno sounds much more normal! Or even Blaunau Festiniog, while Piddletrenthide sounds extraordinary.

It was raining and I needed a B road with four numbers and I couldn't find it.

I stopped and looked at the map and received a small bundle of eagerness on my lap, licking my face and being thoroughly unhelpful. She nosed her tracking harness and dumped it in my lap. 'Oh, Chita, you are a nut!'

I thought I knew where I went wrong so I reversed and found a tiny notice saying Dog Trials, on the wrong side of the road, if you came from the direction

I had come from. People often don't seem to think of us coming from all four corners of the country.

It was just beginning to be light; a grey dismal light creeping up over the grey dismal moors. There were dirty sheep, with unkempt fleeces, looking remarkably tatty after the Suffolk crosses with their plush coats that are a part of my daily life, in the field across the river, and the field beside me. Their black faces and legs are endearing.

Down a long deserted lane, past a derelict farmhouse, the barns broken and empty, rafters bare to the sky. Low stone walls, and flinty lanes.

There was a notice on a gate.

Secretary. It looked fairly improbable if you stopped to think.

Two farmhouses side by side, one occupied and one part of a security business, so that when I went in I found what looked like a TV sheriff's set-up, with the secretary sitting at a table in a cage meant for a guard dog; no dogs were there. They were outside. It was extremely cold and very bare and uncomfortable; a cooker for dog food, and little else. I was offered a cup of coffee in a minute; I was early, it was only a quarter to seven.

There was nowhere to sit, but the coffee was hot and good.

I was to track at 8 a.m. in field 4, which was about a mile back down the lane on the left-hand side. I could take the car and park it at the side of the lane.

The routine was new to me and unfamiliar. At Obedience shows you get your number on a card and pin it to you. Trials don't bother with such niceties; I had to remember I was number 57 in one stake and number 53 in the other; and I was going to confuse them so I wrote stake and number on the back of my hand, which everyone seemed to do.

The loo was outside, behind the barn. The barn had fallen down, so you climbed over rubble to reach a small cubicle with, rather amazingly, a glass half-door. It was necessary to shout your intentions in advance if you weren't to be surprised. The facilities were as primitive as the barn itself. One of the dubious joys of shows and trials in the middle of nowhere is that the countryside seldom produce civilized sanitation though occasionally at an agricultural show you find a caravan fitted up like a royal boudoir.

I sat in the car till ten to eight, watching the sky lighten; there was a flurry of snow. I drank some coffee from my flask and ate some of my lunch, feeling I had been up for hours. I had been up for hours. I had driven nearly one hundred miles as well. And it wasn't yet eight in the morning.

Chita put her nose into my neck and sighed deeply. Bored.

I switched on the radio and switched it off fast as I heard the voice of a politician I would dearly like to send to the Antipodes. Somewhere hot, anyway.

Rule one for all trackers and searchers, and in fact any competition, before you do anything, empty your dog.

It's a pity the dogs can't read.

It's never easy in a strange place with new smells. Chita was enchanted by the ditch and found everything a dog could find there; smell of rat and stoat and weasel and fox; smell of rabbit and hare and smell of birds that foraged there. 'Isn't it exciting?' her body said as she dived from delicious smell to delicious smell, had a quick snack of grass and just when my patience was wearing thin, remembered what I was telling her.

'Sorry, I forgot.'

I suspect the dog equivalent of 'Whoops, sorry,' is written in dog language on Chita's brain.

She leaped at me and licked me, which I didn't want either and sobered her down, as more cars were now arriving and people were walking far more seemly dogs, far more experienced dogs, and there was I once more, the newcomer with a dog like that.

Time to track.

Field 4 was well back down the lane and it was a remarkably scruffy field with scrub grass; it had obviously been occupied for a very long time by a great number of sheep. I looked at the fouled ground and knew we were sunk before we began. I had never tracked with her in a sheep field.

Nor it seemed later did they farm as my farmer opposite does. Even now as I write he is doing his daily inspection; the dogs are working and the sheep filing past the two men, each being inspected as it goes.

However, there were the two poles that showed the start of our track and it was time to put on Chita's harness.

She was wild with excitement, sniffing the sheep-droppings, leaping into the legs of the harness, refusing to listen to my voice. I put my hands on either side of her head and gave her a little shake. 'Behave, *you*,' I hissed at her and she was still for long enough to get her into the harness and to get the line flung free behind me.

I thought it more than likely that, in a field like that, the track-layer had his boots well plastered with sheep muck and the track would be rich with scent; also it might not be clear as the whole field was rich with scent. Added to the sheep were hares and rabbits, their offerings everywhere.

Chita set off at top speed; I leaned back on the rope but there was no way I could hold her, and if I checked her hard she would stop tracking; better to do it fast and lose points there than not to do it all. It was nothing like her normal style.

Fast along the stone wall; was she right? Fast at the corner and down towards the far end of the field and then I caught a whiff of something distinctly unpleasant on the wind. So did she. She didn't think it unpleasant, 'Cor, what's *that*?'

She stopped tracking and stood, head up, scenting the wind that was blowing strongly, again with a hint of snow. The wind was as cold and vicious as malice.

I was glad I had gloves on for two reasons; without them the rope would have burned my hands; and without them my hands would have been blue with cold. The two thoughts came together and I made myself concentrate as now Chita was forging ahead, pulling to the wall. She wasn't tracking and I didn't know what she was doing.

A minute later I did as we reached an extremely dead lamb. It was about a month old, and had been there for at least a day and a night, if not longer, huddled into the angle of the wall, well torn about by foxes, crows, and anything else that hunted high on the lonely moors.

It shouldn't have been there at all and my dog had never smelled anything so lovely before. I remembered Janus finding a washed-up sheep on the beach; he rolled on the carcase, and I had to drive him home. Phew!

Chita fought me, pulling to the sheep.

'Want it. Want it.'

Back to where we left the track and put her head down.

'Want that lamb.'

Back to the track and this time she sighed deeply and shot off and I knew at once she wasn't on the track, but was after bits of sheep tossed around by crows. I found a small cap off a plastic jar and hoped it was the end of the track; I picked it up and showed it to the judge. It wasn't what we were supposed to find.

'What *is* your dog up to?'

I took him and showed him.

'She should learn to ignore things like that.'

I looked at him rather blankly, as it had never occurred to me to track her in a field fouled by sheep, or to lay carcases all around for her to ignore. I wasn't even sure where I would find a carcase; I could put down bits of meat, I supposed, but it seemed a pointless exercise.

The gap between townsfolk and country people is bigger than one realizes.

I wondered what kind of farmer left dead sheep around.

We had to search in the same field.

A twenty-five yard square with four articles in it.

Chita did her busybody walk which meant that she was not going to search at all. Fast racing legs, round

152

and round, head in the air, 'I'm going to that sheep.'

'Chita, here. I want it.'

'I'm going to get it, aren't I? Of course you want a bit of sheep, anybody would.'

She set off again, busy body rushing back to that heavenly smell.

I put on my best no-nonsense voice which I have learned with Chita. I suspected it astounded both the judge and the tracklayer. Shrieking harridan – such a *little* dog! For her breed anyway – she's a giant compared with a Papillon or a Chihuahua. 'Chita, behave!'

I called her to me, sat her and gave her a fierce, hissing lecture.

'Search, you little horror; and leave that sheep alone; now, *I want it.*'

I indicated the square and she decided she would search the square and bring me what I wanted.

It was full of what any sane owner would want.

'Good girl,' I said as I dropped the hard dried sheep-dung in front of me; she had searched, she had brought a trophy and after all, it was more than possible that everything smelled of sheep-dung by now; it was windy and everyone's shoes were filthy; you couldn't navigate properly; there wasn't time to look where you put your feet.

When time was up I had a neat little pile in front of me and no articles. No marks at all, not even for my handling of her, which was admittedly odd; I knew all she wanted was to get at that carcase, but apparently no other dog would have done; or else they were all so brilliantly trained they would ignore it.

I went back to the car, and consoled myself with more coffee.

Then I took my sheet of no marks back to the cottage.

'What happened?'

'There was a dead sheep in the field,' I said forlornly.

'A dead *what*?' said a voice from the corner. 'Why wasn't it reported, where is it, which field? Come and show me on the map.' I pointed to our field and he rushed out. Somebody should have told him.

It was too late for us.

Later, chatting, I found I could sort out those of us who live in towns and those who live in the country by their reactions to my story. Without exception the country people accepted that a sheep should not have been left in the field; that the track should not have been laid in that field, even if it meant that I did not track at all, and that no experienced dog would ignore such a trophy.

Even police dogs when searching are attracted by dead birds or animals in the hedges and ditches and have to be taken on away from the scent; it is overpowering, calling to long-ago instincts that only lie skin-deep and are never forgotten.

Put our dogs loose in the hills and they would soon turn sheep and rabbit killers to survive. Maroon any of us on a desert island and we would soon be combing the ground and the lakes for food; all our civilized habits forgotten in the need to live.

It's always necessary when working with the dog to know the dog; not to know the theory behind the dog. For one thing, no dog is like any other; and when I say Chita is unique, I don't mean it in any way other than the truth. She is not an easy dog to train because she is so alive and so full of her own desires; but Janus is unique in his way and wasn't easy to train and Bob is learning about another golden retriever dog. He wasn't very polite about Titus's stubbornness the other day. I knew exactly how he felt.

My next dog will be unique – and quite different to any of these. Your dog is unique and nothing like any other dog ever born. I'm unique too – and so is every one of us. No carbon copies.

Of necessity when working alone at a new hobby, one is often reduced to reliance on books as no one else does the same thing as you near enough to you; and you tend to work by books. But the writers of the books have never had your dog or my dog; only their own dogs and what works for one doesn't necessarily work for another.

You can't do the same thing in the same way with every dog.

There are dogs you can't be firm with; which 'die' on you. There are dogs you must be firm with or they deride you. There are dogs that remain sweet and gentle all their lives but you can't ever teach up to a high standard as they can no more do the work required than can some children work to get a Ph.D. It isn't a fault; it's a difference. I doubt if Harvey Smith would have been a success as a ballet dancer; or an opera singer; but that doesn't prevent him being top of his own field.

Nobody expects their child to be as good as the boy next door at the same things, and some of those of us with dogs resent it because they don't do as well as other people's dogs.

Why?

I have learned long ago to accept that I can write about my own interests and write well about them, and appeal to my readers, but I don't expect to be read by university dons, or those who prefer a really rattling story of mayhem and murder, or of spies and terrorists or of plagues and disasters. Or professionals in the dog world. I'm not aiming at them – I'm writing for people who, like me, have dogs for pleasure.

Chita is a dog on her own; so is your dog, and there are things she can do that no other dog will ever do; and things your dog can do that mine never will; there are awards to be won by all of us, but it's necessary to find out first just what we can do, and what the dog can do, and do what is possible to the best possible standard.

Last night, talking to Bob, he commented that it's necessary, when out with the dog, to watch every movement; watch it running free, watch how it reacts to commands; does it ignore them, or respond by a look, or come fast? How does it behave on its own, searching the field; what does it do with its spare time? And when you know your dog backwards you use those observations to help you teach it.

Yours loves coming fast for a cuddle? O.K., then teach her to come fast for a cuddle; working on what she loves doing.

Chita loves jumping through long grass looking for 'mouse'. O.K., then let her have fun looking for 'mouse' and in between give her one or two real searches.

Chita is quick to respond to signals, so use signals.

Now Janus is deaf, which happens to a lot of old dogs, I am thankful I always have used both voice and signals as I can put him 'down' or in a 'sit' or bring him to me by hand signals, provided his head is the right way round. If it isn't, there is little I can do if he is at a distance.

With Puma it had to be all voice once she was blind; get the tone right so that she knew it was meant for *her* and not the other two. 'Puma, come,' and she would home in on my voice, running at speed.

If I had managed to teach her to ground-track instead of air-tracking, her life might have been easier when she could no longer see, but she had to depend on the wind. I never did succeed, even with a liver trail, in getting her nose on the ground; she didn't think that way.

Put down ten cloths on the ground, one with my scent on, and she went straight to it, ignoring the rest, not even sniffing them. She had a remarkably good nose in that way; and remarkably good hearing. She could hear sounds inaudible to the other dogs, which sometimes made her edgy as she grew less able to see; she barked at things she didn't understand and distant sounds here can come from the railway, or fire sirens, or the warning noises to ships at sea, booming on foggy days.

We know so little about the dog's world. We have to guess so much and unless we know our own dogs, we haven't a hope of succeeding with them, as we will always do the wrong things for that dog.

I do know now that to train Chita in the way some

books say is to ask for disaster. I have gone back to scratch, forgetting what the books say, using bits of them to guide me, but none of the writers had my dog. Though I still need the books, I have been using them wrongly, as patterns rather than guides.

I know Chita so much better now than I did two and a half years ago; I know how she learns; I also know that she learns fast and forgets fast, and there is no way at all that I can take her at the speed I want, or the speed some other dogs go at.

We go at her speed.

When we can prove that something can be done right and she understands it perfectly, we can go on. We can get full marks for agility; she understands that and has learned how to do it for herself.

That is what I need all the time to remember with Chita.

She must use her own brains; never mine.

At the end of the day we are a team; not one to command and one to obey, because that is never her way. She will do it now because she wants to please me, not because I want her to do it.

That is a very different exercise to teach.

Chapter Nine

One of the difficulties of having a strange hobby is the lack of people to share with. I longed for someone else interested in tracking, and had almost given up hope of anyone nearer than Edith and Bob, both busy with their own work, both (well of course, being married to one another!) nearly forty miles away.

Then Lesley and Reg joined the club with their young Dobermann.

Lesley was willing to learn about tracking. And Rudi needed training, being full of himself, a gorgeous dog, with a coat that shines like a conker.

'The farmer next door to me says we can use his two fields if we want to track,' Lesley said one day, and it was like being given the crown jewels, except you can do a lot more with a field to track in!

Lesley lives at the end of a long lane to nowhere; if you follow the lane past the point where the cars can't go, you come into a deep banked gully between walls and hedges, ending in a field gate. Look over the fields and down to the Straits and across to the dark ever-changing mountains; beyond are sheep and cattle.

The lane is guarded by a retired drug-squad dog, a very old yellow Labrador, who ambles up and barks at us, and because most of our tracking there was done before the fields grew high with hay, I still had Puma who resented a dog barking at her and bayed back at him, unable to see who he was. Janus joined in; and Chita of course raced round the back of the car and then, unable to contain her fury at the intruder any longer, seized her rug and shook it as if she were killing a rat.

I don't like her doing it; as apart from anything else it often hits me on the back of the head and hurts and it infuriates both other dogs. I would drive on, hoping the old dog would give up and go home, or I could stop and chase him off and settle my furious trio. I was never sure what was best to do and it was a good day when the old fellow wasn't there. He is well over thirteen years old and a slow mover at the best of times, and he loves to wander up and down the lane.

Tracking with Lesley proved fun for a number of reasons, not the least because it might be enlivened by Becky and Pod. Becky is a very pretty young donkey whose idea of dealing with Chita is to kick up her hind legs and bray; Chita barks, and we have to settle both animals. Pod is a goat; his idea of fun is to butt if you are within reach and I prefer not to be. He comes to nose the gate and look at us. Recently we solved that problem. Neither Chita nor Rudi like the new electric fence designed to stop the goat from going walkabout.

The other two occupants of the field are Nigel and Flossie, the geese.

Anyone who has encountered geese knows what that means; Nigel puts his head down, his neck outstretched, his wings flapping, apparently about to take off into our faces, defending his mate with his last breath, making that horrible uncanny goose noise that is enough to terrify anyone, let alone the dogs. It takes me back to a farmyard walk long ago when we watched Kenneth take off with a gander flying after him. He made good time that day and at least he did draw the attack away from his family!

Nigel spends much of his time chasing off imaginary raiders. Flossie lays eggs, and Becky lies on them, and nobody is sure whether it is an accident, or a misplaced conviction that she is actually a goose and not a donkey and is wanting to help Flossie hatch her brood. Needless to say, Becky leaves only memories of goslings behind her and Flossie is constantly deprived of motherhood.

That doesn't stop Nigel from defending the eggs he is sure are still there.

Lesley lays a track and later Chita and I follow it. This worked well till one afternoon when we were to track, rather ambitiously, an hour after the track was laid. Lesley would lay it at two, on a damp summer afternoon, when scent would lie well, with the sky overcast so that there was no sun to dry it out; and we would come at three. We arranged it by 'phone.

We arrived at ten to three and Lesley took me into the cottage; we looked through the window and there in the field, happily unaware that the poles had any significance, was a man with four cheerful labradors, racing round, picking up Chita's articles and also the reward that waited for her at the end.

The other field was full of frisky bullocks, so that was the end of that.

I took each dog for a walk, down through the bracken and along the little overgrown footpath, each sniffing blissfully at new smells; Janus zigzagging from one delight to another, sniffing ecstatically and then cocking his leg; Puma, as always going from side to side of the lane, her head in the air, her nose almost touching my hand, careful not to lose touch.

She had lost me one day on the beach when she found a smell on the sand and followed it, as always nose well up, but obviously on the trail of some creature. The wind was blowing from her to me and she couldn't smell me or the other two who were hunting behind her, with me watching carefully as Janus loves to roll in dead fish and nothing smells quite like dead fish, except possibly when the pigs have been through the place and left large traces of their going; that is delicious if you are Janus! We don't share his pleasure.

Puma on that day circled, crying, and I had to get round the other side of the wind and call her, before she could find me. She never left my side after that.

That was the day I knew she could see very little. She fooled us at home as she knew her way round so well and as long as we kept the rooms unchanged she never blundered; she did get worried if visitors came and moved chairs. Both of us had adapted to Puma without even realizing we were doing so.

Now in the lane Puma was in heaven as the smells were all new to her. She nosed my hand, totally content.

Lesley had made coffee, and I joined her indoors, sitting on the floor with Rudi, who had an enormous bone and was chewing it, his mind on the job and not on us.

Visiting Lesley there is a treat in store always, as she has a polecat-ferret.

Out comes Lodie, a delightful animal, with a fluffy body, a dark-marked mask, and eyes full of mischief. He looks like a cross between a weasel and a fluffy otter, and since he loves dens and the room offers lots of opportunity to find them, his advent is always a source of considerable amusement.

Rudi has to go on lead, as for him a polecat is a toy and Lodie is far from happy about that.

Lodie is not usually out in the afternoons and is determined to make the most of it. The room is enormous, the two rooms of the cottage having been made into one. The bedroom is being built, so one end of the room is sitting-room, the other is bedroom, and Lodie careers along the floor, stopping to investigate my wellingtons. He gets inside one and can't turn round and has to come out fast, backwards; he has another look, going right down to the toe, but it lacks something; possibly he hopes for prey inside. Or a titbit.

He pushes it over in disgust and gets under the bookcase and looks at us, planning his next move, which is a sudden sortie across the room and under the bedspread where he runs round in circles. Rudi is fascinated by the swiftly moving hummock, now here, now there, now disappearing as Lodie dives down the side of the bed, only to run again and show us how busy he is.

He emerges, dives across the room, leaps backwards in dismay at nothing, reaches Lesley and burrows into her lap, then decides to investigate me. He comes suspiciously, sniffing every inch of me, his odd musky smell very strong. He sniffs my hands and arms, down my legs, ventures to stand with his paws on my shoulder and very gently, sniffs my hair. He climbs on my lap, not difficult as I am still sitting on the floor close to the fire, enjoying a coal blaze.

He is back with his games again, circling the room fast. He is probably over seven years old; nobody quite knows as he was inherited from somebody else. He made the vet's day memorable when he had to have a tooth out as he is the only polecat-ferret on their books and he is a favourite patient, being unusual, gentle and funny, with an undying curiosity about life in general and the human race in particular. He has never known the wild. He is an indoor animal, living his life out in rooms and a cage.

It is time to go home. I go out to the car, and at once the dogs are all over me; Puma in particular used to scent every inch of me, her eyes closed, her expression blissful. 'What have you been doing? What animal is that? What do you smell of?'

Puma never tracked with her nose to the ground, but she always came to 'read' me when I came home, in a detailed exploration that the others never do. Both of them, oddly, come to smell, not my clothes, but my breath, to see what I have been eating! Puma wanted to know where I had been. She was never as greedy as they are, but she stole and once we had a very odd anniversary dinner as Puma ate two of the tournedos. I'd forgotten how high she could reach.

Sometimes I spent my time with puppies. Nothing is more fun than to be with a litter when they are near to being sold; they are busy, happy, exploring everywhere, coming to you to find out how you behave, pushing eager bodies into your arms, playing with your shoelaces, racing off with any piece of your property you are unwise enough to put down.

After a visit such as this, Puma would be first to meet me.

'Puppies. I remember puppies. Puppies, you've been near puppies.' Her expression changed, becoming dreamy-eyed and broody, and she would put her head against me, so obviously remembering that time in her life when, although she hadn't been too keen on her litter, she had obviously had her maternal instincts

162

triggered for the rest of her life.

Puma always came into club with new puppies; if they were alarmed by the big room, by the big dogs and the big people, they would be put in a corner with Puma beside them and at once she began to mother them. She would check them carefully from nose to tail to make sure they were clean; she would then cuddle up against them, holding them close and protectively between her front paws, and I was reminded of her own mother, who had held each pup upside down on her paws and cleaned it up devotedly.

Witch has been dead a long time now. She too was a very sweet bitch.

Her name used to cause the funniest problems.

'What's her name?' 'Witch.' 'That bitch over there.' 'Witch.'

'*No*, what's her name?'

'Her name is Witch.'

It is odd meeting Puma's breeder now, as I know none of her dogs. The old ones have gone and the new youngsters are unfamiliar, though I have met one or two in the past two years. We very rarely meet, as we live too far away. Just occasionally at a show, or a Trial. Twice in the past three years. Letters at Christmas; the days when I walked her dogs seem very far away, a lifetime away; a lifetime for a dog.

Janus doesn't come in with pups. He doesn't like them one bit and stands there, wrinkling his lips, as they obviously have thoughts of swinging on his ears or tail, or playing scattily around him. He no longer wants to play much with Chita, though in the evening, just before bed, both are triggered to the 'eating' game, that ends when Chita gets too excited and bounces at him, barking, and he lumbers off to his bed, his whole body saying 'Behave little bitch. I'm an old man now.'

His eyes look at me, anxious: 'Get her under control, do. I'm tired.'

He spends a lot of his time in his bed now; getting up is sometimes a bit of a bore, though if I show him a slice of brown bread he is out of bed fast, barking hopefully.

And he still won't have cats on his territory, which does keep him moderately busy as our fields attract visiting cats, who are often to be seen making their way home with mice in their mouths. Yesterday he broke the record and chased a black cat off our field, showing a remarkable speed for his age.

We wish the cats would make war on the moles.

The moles on our ground are prolific and extremely industrious. They have been fought for over five years with the gas that comes from bad eggs (Kenneth used to be a research chemist, and it is easily made and only produces a bad smell and not death); and with various mole-smokes, also designed to remove the moles.

None of them work. All that happens is that infuriated moles kick up even bigger and better molehills within yards of our last site of attack. Chita makes her own small war, which does not involve catching moles; though once or twice she has seen a ripple in the ground and had an infuriated dig, ending up baffled because there is that interesting smell down there, and nothing comes to view. A mole can burrow so fast it's almost unbelievable; it vanishes in seconds.

'Chita, dig,' was a command I used when she was younger, and it always produced the result I wanted; the molehill scattered over the grass. But if she meets a molehill on a track she stops to dig, so I have had to rethink that one. Instead we pass the molehills as we 'work' over and over again, and she must ignore them. Then, when I release her and she is given the command, she may dig.

It has become very plain through the years that to give a dog of her type intensive training (and by that I do not mean harsh training) is to give her a framework for security.

Our own code of manners is very similar. I was brought up to trust people, to believe that they were telling the truth, and to behave as if each day were my last and tomorrow would be judgment day. My father was something of a Puritan; my headmistress, who terrified all of us, including, I believe, her staff, was a Quaker and a very great lady indeed. She left her mark on all of us who came under her care; and I was at her school for seven years. She had a great deal to do with her Sixth Form, and we knew exactly what was expected of us, which in the days just before World War II, was a format for living that made life a great deal easier than it is today.

We were disciplined, never by canes, though we might find an irritated teacher suddenly giving us a rap over the knuckles with a ruler. We had a great deal more fun than children have today; we had to make our own amusements. I used to write plays which we acted for our parents and on one occasion I wrote one for my father's birthday, which was in August.

Our dog had a part in it. That was our Airedale cross, Turk. He came everywhere with me, though he wasn't much of a protector as when we met danger I had to protect him!

I can't remember much about the play, but we were at the seaside. I think in Cromer, where we took a house for a month. We also had a beach-hut and the beach-hut was the stage. To my parents' embarrassment we attracted as much attention as a Punch and Judy show and the play was awful. I was about eleven years old then, and it was hotch-potch of the pantomimes I had seen and the books I had read and I was a romantic child, always in my imagination a boy. I hated being a girl – life then was very restricted for female children. I loathed dolls, sewing, knitting and pretty clothes, preferring shorts and jerseys.

One of my favourite poems at that time was 'Barbara Ritchie' – or some similar title; I haven't seen the poem since and can't remember who wrote it. It is about the American Civil War, and at one point the general (don't write and tell me I am wrong; it's a long time ago that I read it!) says:

Who touches a hair of yon grey head,
Dies like a dog. 'March on,' he said.

I loved saying that, and bored the family to distraction with it, as well as with some of the more gruesome bits of the *Ancient Mariner*. I still like poems with a swing and a swirl to them and have a very unfashionable liking for Kipling, not so much what he says as how he says it.

So that the most effective line in my play, written at the mature age of eleven, was, 'Die, you dog', which had an unexpected effect and convulsed the audience. My brother made an awful mess of dying too. I have no idea what the rest of the play was about. My brother was a pest as a little boy, three years younger than me. He is now a dignified doctor!

Somehow, though I am often asked to write about my early childhood, there is nothing to write about except my experiences with animals. Our family had a strong leaning towards the living world; my brother now a doctor, one of my father's sisters was also a doctor in the days when women doctors were a rarity, as he was born at the end of the last century. Several of my aunts were nurses and my mother I think would have made a great animal nurse, as well as a human nurse. She nursed our black cat through cat 'flu in the 1930s when there were no antibiotics or inoculations and most cats died. Nipper not only survived, but lived for many years afterwards. I can still remember him in my sister's doll's treasure-cot, tucked up warmly, a hot-water-bottle well wrapped up with him.

Now when I visit my mother, she stands in the garden with doves all round her, waiting for her to fill the waterbowls which are always there for them; they have no fear of her at all.

I learned early in my life that animals do not fear you if you keep quite still. People who say they can do anything with animals are sometimes surprised as they are either bitten, or the animal runs off.

When a new puppy comes to class I ignore it. We sit on the floor and talk; or I pass casually and he is intrigued because he is being ignored. Fuss him and he will back off. Children are the same. I never grab my grandchildren and kiss them when they first arrive. If they want to kiss me, they come; if they feel shy of a grandmother who lives a long way away and whom they see rarely, then I wait and talk to their parents, and it isn't long before I find a small person cuddling against my knee, waiting to be lifted on to my lap, just to be held tightly.

People often think I don't like children; I do. But children prefer not to be fussed; like dogs, they will make their own approach; and being sensible little people, they are wary until they are sure they can trust you. Also I prefer to treat them as equals – they are far more sensible than some people think, and understand more than parents realize.

Trusting is not a matter of spoiling. The dog must know his place in the family, which is right down at the bottom of the pack. I was called to task by one reviewer for saying my three are a pack; they should be a family. A family *is* a pack; father and mother are pack leaders, and the children are kept in their place in the pack, in a well-run home. This is not bullying or throwing an adult's weight about; it is the only way in which knowledge and experience can be passed. In the wild it helps keep the inexperienced babies safe from wolf and tiger, eagle and buzzard – a disobedient youngster dies.

The old wolf is the pack leader, always; often a female. In the deer herd the barren grandmother is usually the leader of the herd; it is her wisdom and her past experience that warns the new babies that there is fire in the forest; they have never smelled fire; she has not only smelled it, she has suffered it and her fear stampedes them; they don't know why, but next time they smell smoke they will run without being told. They have learned from the leader.

She knows that the fox can kill a weakly fawn; and she will alert the herd, so that they ring round the baby and may, in some cases, trample the fox to death.

The dog in a well-run family is part of a well-ordered pack and knows the rules; and knows too the way the family lives so does not die under cars, or by falling over a cliff, or by drinking disinfectant.

Chita knows the household routine so well that she can lead me through it, and only recently did I realize that she does just that. When we have no visitors we have slipped into a familiar pattern; on fine days Kenneth gardens, which takes a lot of time with two acres to keep mown, even if only roughly mown, and the vegetable patches to look after; and there are always household jobs.

I write in the mornings. That is an almost unvarying rule. So she leads me to my study and takes her place, curled up by the open door where she can keep one eye on me. If the 'phone rings, she is up, telling me with her eyes that I have to go and answer it.

I can't race there or she gets too excited. I have to slow myself down with Chita. 'Softly, softly, little lady,' and if she gets too wild I have to sit her and put my hands on her head. 'Now, what's all this about? Calm down. No hurry, nothing to fuss about; gently, girl, gently.'

Now she understands and sits with her ears back, her brown eyes gazing into mine, with a doe-eyed expression that reminds me of Puma's 'I smell puppy' look. We go on, either out into the garden or to the car, or to answer the 'phone, and she has remembered she must not go wild. She still can, very easily, if I don't watch, which is why she only stays with people who know her well, who understand her and whom she respects. She would never dream of playing Kenneth up though he has little to do with the dogs; he expects them to behave and they know it and do.

Even during the early part of the day Chita knows the routine; she is waiting at the door of the room where she sleeps with Janus when I open the door. They greet me as if I have been away for years; there is nothing quite like being greeted by one's own dog to start the day well. Unless it's to be greeted by a purring cat.

Then they lead me to the utility-room door, and wait

for it to be opened. The biscuit-box is there, and the door to the garden. They watch me as I lift the biscuit-box to the top of the deep-freeze, open the door and let them out. They have both been taught to empty on command, and the magic word produces the desired result. With Janus now, I have to show him a biscuit to remind him why he has gone out as he doesn't always remember. A hedgehog passed in the night; or the partridge babies have just run from the nest and he wants to sniff it. His biscuit reminds him and he comes in and sits by Chita, who is already waiting for her reward, knowing she must sit before she gets it, so anticipating the command.

Biscuits given, it is time to feed the cat and both dogs watch as I put out her Weetabix and tinned milk as for some reason ordinary milk upsets her; she can take diluted evaporated milk without trouble and I don't give any of my animals meat alone as it does strain the kidneys; they need cereal too.

When cat (who is noisy till she has her food) is put outside the door to eat away from dogs, dogs know it is time for our breakfast and go without telling to their beds. Before we sit down to eat Chita is at the door to finish off what cat has left, and bring me the plate to wash.

It is at this point she will tell me if the dogs' water-bowl is empty and slam it against the refrigerator hard, lapping at nothing, then looking at me to make sure I know she is trying to get water from an empty bowl. Once it is filled she is happy and goes again to her bed. Janus grumbles at the empty bowl.

If I forget any part of the routine, I find Chita has stuck to it. If I don't have a bath, which I normally do when I get up, I find her standing in the bathroom looking thoughtfully at the bath taps. 'Why have you forgotten?'

She only has to see me go to the shelf where we always put our car keys, as we are otherwise both dab hands at losing them, to know we are going out, and she stands by the car. If I have brought in her tracking harness to clean, and pick it up, she is convinced we

169

are going to track; though it is kept in the car, and she might be wrong.

If I remove the dirty linen from the basket she is waiting at the foot of the stairs and leads the way to the utility-room where the washing-machine is kept. She watches, fascinated when I am podding peas, or peeling apples; she can link an apple to the knife-drawer as I don't like the skin and if I pick up an apple, she surprises me by trotting out to the drawer as if to say, 'Come on, that's what you need now.' She watches a new procedure intently, trying to understand what I am doing.

She is very aware of signals, so much so that she has to have very definite ones or she misinterprets. She watches my hands; and before I know it she has done something I intended her to do a few seconds later and I was just working out when to give her the command.

She still has her own zany sense of humour; little clown, though I am not sure whether it is to amuse me, or to defy me; only yesterday I ordered her to hurdle. She yo-yo'd, over and over, without stopping, and came to me with a mischievous look in her eyes. 'How about that then?'

She got a tiny shake and a 'Bad girl, now do it right.'

'O.K.' she said with all her body and did a perfect hurdle and went 'down' when I told her instead of running back to me. And before I told her to move had raced to the scale, gone over that and back and come to lie at my feet while I was still summoning my breath to tell her to behave. She is so fast she is misnamed; she could be called Mercury (Quicksilver). She would also make a good messenger for the gods, as she would run like the wind.

But defiance, even if funny, can't be allowed; it could lead to dangerous tricks like jumping the wall and running off; and refusing to come back when I call her. So she comes on the lead for a few minutes and then we go back to the hurdle and scale and long-jump and I get a perfect response.

'Good girl, aren't I?'

'Sometimes.'

Much more often now.

Now I find myself saying much more often, 'Clever girl, aren't you clever?' Her tail wags, her eyes laugh at me and she leans against me. 'Yes, I'm clever!'

And out we go for more training.

Training is never straightforward. Chita was doing extremely well and we had made immense progress with her 'stays', and she was becoming far more secure, when we had another setback – this time a remarkably annoying one, which upset her confidence considerably, so that once more I was back to retraining her to stay.

I was driving to visit friends when a motor-cyclist skidded on the corner, coming towards me. His bike sailed through the air and crashed against the dogs' door and broke their window; his helmet hit my door, as I had fortunately seen it happen and had been able to turn sideways into a luckily placed lane and prevent him coming straight through the windscreen.

Neither of us was badly hurt, though we must both have been shocked, because as he picked himself up, he said forlornly, 'I've hurt my thumb,' and held it out to me like a little boy wanting it bandaged and we both started to laugh and couldn't stop.

The dogs were all asleep and woke on impact. Puma banged her head; Janus began to bark and wouldn't stop and Chita sat up, and then she too barked. I don't know if she hurt her head.

They settled down when we got to our friends, as I was almost at my destination. We checked the dogs, and they gave me a cup of hot sweet tea and I relaxed for an hour before driving home.

That night I went into the kitchen as I was getting the dogs' food, I put the lid on the kettle. Metal against metal; all three dogs bolted. It was several weeks before they could come into the kitchen with metal noises there; though it is now forgotten.

What is not forgotten is that they woke to see a motor-cyclist's helmet against the broken window of the car and they bark at motor-cyclists behind our car now; which can be a great nuisance. It was months before I stopped saying to myself as a motor-cyclist approached me, 'Please don't skid.'

It hadn't been his fault; it was a dreadful day, the rain teeming down; the road newly surfaced, with loose chippings. I had realized on the corner before that the road was a death-trap and we were both going very slowly. His wheels just didn't go round the corner, which was already marked with skid tracks. Luckily he was an ambulance driver and very well protected with the best motor-cycling gear. If he hadn't been, he would have been dead, as I have never heard anything like the crack as his head hit the window; the window was broken clean in two. The crack was across the middle and the glass was held in position by the grooves around it. The car needed the whole of one side replaced, and all the windows on that side.

We were both very lucky.

So were the dogs; I still don't know why they weren't badly hurt.

It made a difference to our showing that year, as the car was out of action for some weeks for anything but short journeys. Maddeningly it happened two weeks before our daughter's wedding, which was to be in Birmingham, so I drove over there very carefully in the early morning, as the car was driveable but they hadn't been able to get the parts to repair it, and I was uncertain of its reliability in spite of a thorough going-over. With damaged doors, it didn't feel all that safe; I was a little afraid the locks might have gone and the dogs' door would fly open.

Fortunately it was safe, but I made extra sure by fastening a lead to the handle and attaching it to the back of my seat.

The wedding went off beautifully, with time for me to slip out with the dogs and walk them between the church service and the reception. Not exactly the gear for dog walking! We spent the night in the newly-weds' house, while they went off on honeymoon, which proved slightly complicated as Anne has three cats; and they definitely felt very threatened by our three dogs.

They have a cat-flap which did overtime duty that night. The evening was punctuated by the sound of the trap flapping open, the run of the dogs, a startled hiss and the trap flapping shut again as one cat or the other peered in, discovered dogs and then fled.

The dogs came upstairs at night and the cats came in and slept in peace. They had to be fed in the garden. Friends next door were looking after them in the honeymooners' absence. Anne had bought the house before they married and lived there for a year so she knew her neighbours well.

I think the cats were very relieved when we went. It is still a slight problem visiting as the cats are not used to dogs, and though Anne and Dave have now moved to a bigger house with more garden, there is still a flap for the three cats. To add to the fun, one of her new next-door neighbours has two cats, and there is one cat on the other side, so there are six cats who all have frequent panics as I lead the dogs from the car to the bungalow.

It was only after the wedding that I realized my ribs hurt; my seat belt had prevented me from being thrown out of the car, but the jolt had cracked two ribs. I wondered what it had done to the dogs. Puma had banged her head very hard; I heard the crack, as she hit the window; I have wondered since if that started the trouble that led to her death a few months later, as her behaviour began to change. I hadn't had time to brake. The car was slewed round to face the wrong direction as the bike hit it, so she was flung hard.

Janus is rarely bothered by upsets; he is a remarkably well-balanced, stable dog, and doesn't react to anything much now; he takes all that humans may do to him in his stride; even if small children fall over him, or drop toys on him, or, a far worse crime, sit in his bed! That puzzles him but he sighs and lies down on the rug instead, his attitude saying 'Oh, well, people!'

The car took some time to be repaired; while it was

173

away, I walked with Chita to the farm, and, without thinking, put her on a stay. A motor-bike went past at the end of the lane and she raced to me.

'Motor-bike. Can't stay alone.'

We had already been to two Trials; she had not been good at her stay but she had made an attempt. And she had been in three Obedience shows recently, had come fifth, fourth and third, and had stayed perfectly each time, though admittedly in the Obedience ring I don't go out of sight. But I hadn't gone out of sight on the farm field either; I was only a few feet from her.

I took her home and put her on a 'stay' in our garden; a familiar place that she knows well. She would not relax for a moment. It was like trying to train a pup that had never been taught. I wondered if the accident had damaged her head; I wondered if she had forgotten the rest of the exercises, so I put her through her paces.

No problem at all.

'Chita, STAY.'

Might as well talk to the cat; she won't stay either. Janus meanwhile was lying quiet, and so was Puma.

I rang Edith.

She had a class of difficult dogs every Thursday and if I liked to come over I could put Chita on the stays first with the other dogs and then on her own, while they worked round her, building her up to full confidence again.

Edith's kennels are by the sea, nearly forty miles from here, so I would leave about eight-thirty to be there for ten, and then work till twelve. Outside in the road with five or six other dogs; heeling and turning, sitting and staying, taking it gently, easing her back to confidence.

Stay while the other dogs stayed.

Stay on her own while they worked round her and I stood and watched her.

Stay on her own and leave her for a few moments and return to her, showing her I always came back to her. Making her stay down even when I was beside her, preventing her from leaping up, which could be dangerous for her if cars were coming or some danger threatened as it can. I was once in a bomb scare with Janus and very glad he had been Obedience trained as he did as I told him and was no problem and we were able to get out of the area, which the police were clearing, without causing anyone else any problems either.

Chita had to learn.

Stay while I walked down the road and behind the cafe.

Stay while I walked down the road and hid behind a caravan.

Stay while I walked down the road, and came back beyond the trees, away for nearly five minutes.

She was learning slowly to stay quietly and not move.

And then one morning, we were on the grass, all the dogs in a stay, when a stray dog came running and before I had time to blink, Chita was up, chasing him off, and all our work was undone again. I dropped her and called her and scolded her and she came back, and we started again at the beginning.

Now she needed other dogs appearing unpredictably to steady her; and to stay while the kennel cat came out and teased the dogs; till I seemed to be thinking up new ways of doing the stay and steadying her all the time, and so did Edith.

She has just had a month off; very little formal training, no Trials training; in an effort to try and overcome her worries, and the hope that when we start again we will have overcome this last setback.

I often feel like Robert Bruce's spider; try, try, try again.

With Chita, it seems to apply even more than with either of the other two. I only hope that the Fates don't have any more little surprises in store for us which will set us back again.

There is no way of living without some disasters. Nobody is immune. Only recently one of the best-known German Shepherd breeders, Roy James, died in a motor accident; his wife is going on alone. Beside that, a problem with the stays palls into insignificance. We were very lucky as if that motor-bike had come through the windscreen I wouldn't be here writing this.

Last week we did an agility display with another club and Edith and Bob came over with them. They were delayed by a fatal accident involving a motor-bike and a car, and as Edith told me about it, my mind went back to less than a year ago, when my car was wrecked; and I thought again how fortunate we had been. Another few yards; another minute; and death is as near as that.

So what if Chita won't stay, and I don't ever qualify her?

I remember my father when our house was bombed by a landmine in 1942.

He said, 'So what. We're alive, aren't we?'

And that is what really matters.

Being alive and carrying on, and not being thrown by the idiotic setbacks that nobody can avoid, and not setting undue store on success with our dogs; that's not what they are about.

My little imp is lying by the door watching me; time to get the post; to have coffee, done enough today. Her eyes say it all and off we go, without any knowledge of the future or what it holds in store for either of us, good or bad.

Yesterday she stayed for ten minutes while I stood ten yards from her; without moving, without bothering, without worrying. Maybe we have cracked it now. Maybe tomorrow she will find a new worry; she is that kind of dog.

Whatever she does, it makes life interesting; and who can ask for more than that?

Chapter Ten

Our most recent adventure was a visit to Newcastle to Tyne Tees Television, to be on the programme *A Better Read*. It was a long way; and I am not happy driving in towns, as here we have little traffic.

Also that week I planned to spend touring Herriot country with my friend Joy and her two Shelties and my two dogs, as it was just after Puma's death and I wanted a change of scenery. I missed Puma too much, and we had had a hard time with her, as I should have had her put to sleep early in the year and I kept hoping her symptoms would vanish. But blindness and terror at strangers doesn't vanish; they only get worse.

I hadn't realized, till after she died, how much I protected her.

She came with me everywhere, in case anyone startled her. I was constantly stopping her from barking by saying, 'It's all right Puma, it's only Liz . . . it's only an aeroplane; it's only the helicopter, it's only a cow calving . . .' Everything triggered her to bark when she couldn't see what was there.

And then the other dogs barked too and it was most remarkably noisy.

She barked at sounds in the night; she guarded me when visitors came; she was no longer herself, we know now. It wasn't till I rang Sue who had just lost her bitch through a brain tumour that I recognized what was wrong. I had no option.

Sometimes a dog does behave oddly and brain tumours can be the cause. We have had at least three in the club; and breeds with pushed-in heads, like Boxers and Bulldogs, can also suffer from them. By no means all, just a very few, but any abnormal behaviour needs investigating because the dogs aren't possible to live with, and may get worse.

So Joy and I planned to go away. Then the invitation

came to be on the programme and I had promised my publishers that if it came, this was one engagement I would do.

It was April. The Tyne Tees people promised to find us a hotel for two nights, which would take the dogs. I said we needed gardens for them. Sheila Hocken was to be on the programme with me. I hadn't met her but I had read *Emma and I*. I wondered if she would have Emma. I wondered whether to take Chita with me to the studio. Joy would look after Janus. She was used to my dogs though hers are much smaller. Both are getting on in years and Pepper is almost blind. It was easier without Puma, though I missed her very much. She had taken a great deal of my time as blind dogs need special care and consideration, as do deaf dogs. They need more protection than the normal dog.

Chita needed protecting too as she still was inclined to race after anything that moved fast and though I can drop her on command, I have to see her start or it's too late. She might not behave for Joy, who has never lived with a dog like Chita.

We had lost our holiday as we needed to travel on Tuesday. I was to be at the studio all day Wednesday, and we were to come home on Thursday.

We decided to make a day out of both journeys and explore. We were to come back on the Herriot Trail through Yorkshire, seeing as much as we could, and were to go up via Hadrian's Wall, which neither of us had seen.

We started on a cold grey day, and drove up the motorway. Since neither of us enjoys motorway meals we found a charming pub with good food, and an air of history, and relaxed and ate and enjoyed ourselves, then continued our journey till we came to the Wall. By then the sun was shining.

Our first trip with the dogs was slightly untoward as there were sheep. Joy's two Shelties, being elderly and now fairly staid, trotted at her heels, without a lead; there was no way I dared have Chita off lead with sheep around; I had no idea what she might do and no intention of finding out the hard way; she also still needs a lot of controlling as she is young and brash and lively. Janus, being deaf, could not go off either as he bumbles along for ever on rabbit trails and then stands baffled unable to see me or hear me, a very bewildered expression on his face. And I get more exercise than I need, going after him.

Joy went in front and my dogs decided that the only place to be was with her; and fast, which nearly resulted in a spill for me.

After a few minutes, in which she watched me, and decided she could never live with big dogs, we parted company; she went one way and I walked towards the remains of the old fortifications and stood looking out over the fells; the fields stretched away into the distance, the ruined stones told stories to those who could hear; the sheep grazed on the pasture, and the sky was remote, eggshell blue, and clear.

I sat on the stones and the dogs lay at my feet and the car park was below us, my car a small toy, a child's plaything; nothing was real except the hovering kestrel whose ancestors had no doubt hovered when the Romans guarded these walls.

We met at the car; I trained Chita for a little to get some of the steam out of her and we drove on, to stop again at yet another part of the wall and this time walk without the dogs at Housteads. They were asleep in the car; it was cool, a keen wind blowing and we wandered through the caravan of souvenirs, buying maps, and little gifts; we bought an icecream each and wandered towards the fort, laughing, relaxed, enjoying a change for both of us. Joy has a very busy life, as she takes in three students and very rarely takes a holiday of any length of time.

The Wall stretched along the top of the hill. I walked along the ramparts and looked out over the fields; Joy had a map of the place and we identified various parts of the old fort. The turf was short and springy and there were wild flowers. It was nearly 6.00 p.m. and towards closing time and few people were around.

The world was ours; nobody to share it or spoil it.

When I got back to the car Joy went to read a plaque on the wall and again my notebook came out.

We stood on the wall at close of day
Blue was the sky, though the clouds were grey;
Fields stretched to the hills that were far away.
We stood on the stones where the legions trod,
And walked in the dusk on the dew-drenched sod,
Where an altar was raised to an alien god.
Nothing now moves on the hills but sheep,
Yet green are the memories that men keep,
And green are the graves where the Romans sleep.

We drove on, both of us silent. The four dogs were curled behind us, Chita surprisingly cuddled against Glenn. The countryside is timeless; unchanged by the centuries, though perhaps there were forests then.

I look out from my window now at the fields that rise to the sky. Four Welsh Black bullocks graze our water meadow; a heron has just flown in and is standing in the reeds. It gives a sense of stability. The view was the same in 1804 when Jane Owen lived in our cottage. In the top field is the calf that was born yesterday evening, lying by its mother.

All these things happened when the Romans were here; nothing has changed since then in the animals' world, though perhaps the cattle are very different. Birth and death and the eternal green of the trees and grass have never altered. They would recognize my landscape, even though the doubtful benefits of civilization would puzzle or amaze them.

I would rather lie on the grass beneath the trees and watch the birds than watch television. I would rather walk with my dogs and picnic in the woods than eat in a big hotel. I would rather sit with my cat on my knee than see many of the modern London plays and films. I would rather watch the cattle graze than shop in a big city.

We drove through lanes that led to the motorway again and came into Newcastle, and at once I struck trouble, as it was all one-way streets and the hotel appeared to have vanished.

Luckily everything that goes wrong amuses Joy who is a very good companion, and I smartly followed what we thought was a sign for the city centre and ended up in a rather odd cul-de-sac; we sat there laughing. We had visions of spending the night going round and round Newcastle. I reversed the car and got back on the road again and found somebody had angled the sign wrongly; we followed the road it didn't point to and once more were among traffic and all the busy terrifying mess of the one-way systems in a big place.

Tyne Tees TV had sent us a map. We needed a church as a landmark. We found it and followed the road that led from it. Only it happened to be the wrong church!

We wandered round the one-way system again. My idea of hell is to be in a car in the rain, either on a motorway with no exit or in a one-way system with no exit, with a passenger I don't like who has cadged a lift.

As it was we laughed again and I managed to get back into the system more or less in the right place and Joy asked somebody where the hotel was. He told us. I didn't believe him as we seemed to have to cross the bus lane and into an alleyway and up to the top of the shopping precinct.

And we had to drive round the system yet again.

We did, and passed our guide frantically gesticulating at a narrow alley that could only lead to nowhere; or perhaps to a mugging and a stolen car?

I was tired and the dogs were hungry and even Joy was tired. She always seems tireless.

We had to drive round the one-way system again.

Six times? We'd certainly been round three times, maybe more.

I nosed into the alleyway and to my horror came to a multi-storey car park with a circular ramp and I was very tired indeed and driving an almost new car that didn't corner the way my old car had. I was dizzy by the time I got to the top, but there was the hotel, on top of the shopping precinct.

Where was the grass for the dogs?

All there was was a car park. Nothing at all for dogs.

We looked at one another in dismay.

We were both very tired; it had been almost a two-hundred-mile journey and our lunch hadn't been very adequate and we were starving and I wanted a drink; I don't often drink, but a small one would just fill the bill. Joy agreed enthusiastically.

Meanwhile how did we exercise the dogs?

They had had a long walk, so maybe they would be all right till we had had our meal.

We fed them and went indoors.

Our rooms were on the second floor and both had bathrooms; plenty of room for the dogs. We washed and went up to the bar, and then into the dining-room on the sixth floor.

We were very hungry and I had been told that I would be met next day; so it was with slight dismay that, halfway through our very much desired meal, I heard someone ask if I were around as I was dining with them. Joy and I looked at each other. Had we boobed?

I went and explained and we finished our meal, then joined the people from the programme who were to find out a bit about me and what I did. I was rather tired and felt stupid; but it was an interesting evening.

I always feel out of place in a town because though we lived in a suburb I have never lived a conventional suburban life; I was out in the woods and the parks and the fields, in kennels and on farms and in stables, every day that I could spare. Cheshire is a big county with a lot of horses, cattle, and farms; with kennels and with stables, and there was always somewhere to go.

Wales is no different.

The hotel was stifling and I felt enclosed by walls.

And then the evening was over and what did we do with the dogs?

I looked at my car. There was no way I was going to

brave Newcastle's daunting one-way system, especially at night, until it was time to leave and even then I knew I would get lost. I was right; but neither Joy nor I envisaged anything like the way we did get lost; that, unfortunately, was still in the future. The night porter suggested a taxi to the Town Moor.

The taxi-driver was a little surprised when we piled in with four dogs, but took us to the Town Moor; we walked the dogs and he waited. Those dogs spent the most expensive pennies in Newcastle that any dogs ever spent.

We had to take them out to the Town Moor again early next morning. We were up by seven and by eight were out with the dogs, letting them have a really good walk, as Joy was going to be marooned with them all in her room. There was no way she could walk four of them. I was due to leave for the studio at ten. They had very kindly given me extra time so that the dogs could be exercised. I decided against taking Chita; she was finding hotel life enough to contend with and had never been in a studio; and I was to be there all day. She had never been in a lift before, but soon accepted it. She behaved beautifully, and her manners made us friends who admired her. Janus always makes friends. People may find Alsatians rather alarming.

I dressed myself in a blue trouser-suit, brushed my hair and rather wistfully, left Joy to her knitting and book and the TV set and the dogs and went off to the studio.

Tom Coyne, who had been on Pebble Mill, was to interview us; we had met the night before; and Naomi Lewis who had reviewed some of my books and enjoys animal books was also to be with us; which made it all very easy; and I met Sheila Hocken for the first time. She had with her, not Emma, but Bracken, who rang a bell in my mind as one of my club members, who had, very sadly, died the year before, bred chocolate-coloured Labradors. No, Bracken wasn't one of hers, but Sheila did have one of theirs. It made a small link; it's a small world.

Sheila was more used to TV procedures than I as she had been on a lot of programmes. I had mostly been on programmes like *Look North*, which is only a brief appearance. This was to be slightly longer and much more rehearsed and I found it difficult to keep what I said within the time limits and felt sorry for them as I was so inexpert I must have been infuriating. Sheila was so experienced I felt very awkward and inept.

Also I couldn't come to terms with the battery of cameras and was most disconcerted to find I was surrounded by what appeared to be hundreds of them, and if I turned my head, saw myself behind me, which I found totally unnerving.

Each of us had to talk about the three animal books we had enjoyed most; that alone was difficult to do as we only had a few seconds for each. I had chosen *Tarka the Otter*, which was the first animal book I ever read; *Jack* by Frank Walker which is one of the best dog stories I have ever read, and *Pilgrims of the Wild* by Grey Owl, which is about beavers and I adored it when I was a child.

We rehearsed and rehearsed and then at last it was recorded and we could go to lunch. I needed to escape from the studio as I was developing a headache and knew a breath of fresh air, even briefly, would help. It was daunting to go into a city street and I found myself longing passionately for woods and fields, but we went, Tom Coyne and Mr Hocken and I, to have a drink and talk about current affairs. Television news at least provides everybody with some topic of conversation. We are all much better informed about world affairs these days.

We went back to lunch. I envied Sheila because she had Bracken with her; I am as lost as she is without my dogs. I wished I had brought Chita.

The programme was edited during the afternoon and played through for us and then I went back to the hotel where the dogs went mad. We took another taxi and took them out for a long walk.

It was plain to both of us on these walks that life is

very different for the owners of small dogs and the owners of large dogs. Joy could amble along gently, her two dogs at her heels; my two seemed to be much fuller of life and no way would they settle to a sensible speed.

Both Janus and Chita being dominant also have always been determined animals and if I walk them both I can't fight them both. They do walk beside me, but not at the speed of two elderly Shelties. Even Janus at eleven expects to be off at a much greater speed than that and we kept up a fast pace compared with Joy's more leisurely and relaxed speed.

We had to walk in opposite directions. Janus and Chita found wonderful smells and had to investigate; Chita found other dogs and I had to stop her telling them to get lost; she still has a disconcerting habit of seeing another dog off 'her' territory.

Chita was learning. One day she was lying quiet, the other dogs were working round her, and suddenly a stray black dog came onto the field. No way was Chita going to allow that and she raced at him, telling him where he could go. He went. It had happened so fast that I hadn't the chance to drop her before she reached him, but she did drop and I heeled her. No good scolding her as she had just done what I asked and gone down on the spot.

She was far more biddable provided I saw the other dog first. On another occasion a friend staying with us took his bitch out of the car. I forgot Chita hadn't met her; Chita raced at her, yelling 'Get off my land!' 'Down', I called and she dropped, and I went to her and heeled her with me; after that there was no more trouble.

She did the same thing this year at Working Trials, just before Joy and I went to Newcastle.

Having done her search we went off to play with her quoit and so did an enormous German Shepherd dog. I yelled 'CHITA DOWN' at the top of my voice and she dropped as if she had been poleaxed. I apologized; 'Not to worry,' the other handler said, 'but a good job you did as he would have been very nasty if

185

she had barked at him.'

It might have taught her a lesson; and it might have upset her for life. You never can be sure, with dogs.

So there on the Town Moor I had to watch her all the time, which was another reason for not walking with Joy. We parted company as soon as we got out of the taxi.

I was glad that evening when our walk ended and we could go back to the hotel, as it had been a tiring day. Rehearsals aren't easy and timing everything you say is very difficult; also it is difficult to work with people you don't know at all, as you have to learn about one another, whereas working with those who are familiar to you isn't nearly such a strain. You know what to expect, and this was all very new to me. Though everyone was very kind, which did help a great deal. Television studios are frantic places compared with my quiet study!

We were to join up with the two writers who were on the next day's show during the evening; we had to plan our route for tomorrow, and we ate alone, working out which way we were going. We knew how to get out of Newcastle; we knew which road to take; we also wanted a brief look at the shops before we went. We planned, blissfully unaware that Newcastle still had a surprise in store for us next day, as nobody told us there were two ways out of the car park.

We joined the other party for our coffee.

Naomi Lewis, Sheila Hocken and I were part of the programme on animal books. Mike Ashley, Tanith Lee and Anne McCaffrey were Science Fiction.

Tanith had written the *Blake Seven* programmes. Anne I knew of, as we have the same publisher and I had read and enjoyed some of her books about dragons. I've since read all I can find. Talking to her, I soon found out why as she breeds horses; she rides stallions, and her methods of working with her horses are the same as my methods of working with dogs; her dragons are the ultimate companions, the perfect horse/dog partner, that man can commune with; beautiful creatures that enchant their riders, yet are also animal. I loved talking to Anne and the evening passed too fast.

We went down to get the dogs and were asked to bring them up to the bar, where dogs were allowed. It was easy enough to get the three dogs to spend pennies as there was a pile of earth and a lamppost. Chita was a very different proposition as Chita must have grass; and being Chita she won't compromise.

So I would have to leave Janus while I went off in a taxi with Chita. He might not behave without me.

'Janus is too big to come up,' I said.

'Do bring him. We'd love to see him.' Anne McCaffrey's son was used to big dogs and offered to look after him.

The bar was crowded with people and the tables were low and too close together. Up went Joy with two angelic Shelties; they lay down, having trotted in daintily and made friends with everyone. Up came Janus in the lift. People go to Janus's head. In he went, beaming all over, his tail wagging furiously. Too furiously as he sent Tom Coyne's drink flying into his lap. Tom was charming though I am sure he didn't feel it and I felt dreadful; trust Janus. I went out next morning to buy a book token by way of apology; and hope I won't be remembered for ever as the dreadful woman with that dreadful dog.

Janus settled down at last and I went down in the lift to get Chita out to some grass and then come back. It was snowing when I took her out of the car. Snow – it was almost May. I went into the foyer to find the night man.

'I need a taxi,' I said.

'Now?'

'Please.'

He looked at me, looked at Chita, who was sitting like a small angel, behaving almost too perfectly. I hoped there weren't any cats around; or girls with long dresses who might come too close; or anything that might spark off one of her more lively reactions.

'Where do you want to go?' the night porter asked me.

'Just to some grass,' I said without thinking and without even batting half an eyelid he repeated this to the person on the 'phone.

I heard the reaction halfway across the foyer.

'Look, mate, if you want to be funny . . .'

'Tell him my bitch needs to go out and there isn't any grass here,' I said.

Five minutes later a cab drew up and I went outside. I looked at the driver. He grinned at Chita and patted her.

'I've got a Labrador bitch,' he said, and we drove off into the darkness. I don't know where we went but there was some splendid grass. I have a feeling we were in a very remote corner of the cemetery.

Chita knew why she was there and it was snowing hard and she was as cold as I was. She obliged very fast and ten minutes later we were back at the hotel with snow in her fur and in my hair. I paid the taxi and went up to the bar, where Chita was greeted with pleasure and behaved regally, going from one person to the other, capturing hearts all round, making Janus jealous so that I decided it was time to call it a night and go down to our room. The hotel staff decided the same thing at about the same time as suddenly all the lights but one went out.

The dogs settled down remarkably quickly. They had been fed in the car park several hours before and all they needed was a drink of water.

We decided in the morning it might be well to have a last taxi to the Town Moor, then do our shopping and get off about ten-thirty. Everything went according to plan.

We paid our bill, loaded the car and set off down the alleyway, coming at once to the wrong road, and into that nightmare of a one-way system.

Joy looked at the map. We could follow the Gateshead signs.

We did; to the swing bridge, and then back into the one-way system. We passed Tyne Tees TV studios for the third time and this time I decided we would not follow the Gateshead signs, we would go over the bridge. The signs were at the wrong angle, we then discovered, and we crawled onto the bridge in a long queue that seemed almost stationary. Cars in front of us turned and went back the way we had come; we thought about this; there seemed to be some kind of hold-up, but if we went off where would we end up? At least this way seemed to offer some prospect of getting out of Newcastle and I really didn't think I could face another round trip to nowhere.

We crawled to the middle of the bridge.

We stopped.

People all round us seemed to be out of their cars, smoking and chatting.

I got out of my car and walked to the end of the bridge to find several policemen acting as porters, frantically trying to clear the road of what appeared to be several thousand cartons of food or drink. A lorry had jackknifed and shed its load.

The radio was fairly interesting. We planned the rest of the journey, wondering if we would ever get off the bridge, but at last we were mobile again and crawled past a rampart of boxes, and out on to the road for Yorkshire.

I filled up at a garage and told the attendant our adventures.

One lady it seemed had managed to lose the whole of Newcastle. That, I felt, was quite a feat, as I couldn't get rid of Newcastle. Its one-way system haunted me. I was relieved when we stopped to exercise the dogs in a wood and met somebody else who had a Golden Retriever. Janus and his bitch admired one another and we admired them; and I told them the story of our trips round and round Newcastle.

They had done exactly the same thing.

I began to suspect that people who lay out towns' one-way systems have tortuous minds; or possibly thoroughly sadistic ones. It's easy when you know, but when you don't know, then you can have great fun. Only it does begin to pall.

The woods were delightful.

Joy went off with her dogs, and I walked mine; by now we took it for granted that we didn't go together; it was far better to separate. I enjoyed my active brace, but now I could take one at a time. Joy enjoyed her leisurely jaunt. Chita found all kinds of interesting smells; Janus wandered round in a splendid daze of delight, trotting from one place to another, overcome with pleasure at being out of the car and out with me and somewhere different. He used to hate new places; now he loves them and can never have enough of them.

He found what was probably a squirrel track and we went off into the deep woods.

Chita meanwhile was sitting in the car, telling everyone she had been deserted and nobody loved her and she was FED UP. When Chita is fed up we all hear about it; she sings it at the top of her voice; she scrabbles dementedly at the hatchback trying to open up before I do and I stand back with my arms folded refusing to release her till she shuts up. Finally it dawns on her that she can't win this round and she sits quiet and comes out meekly.

'Of course I wasn't making a noise; I'm ever so quiet, aren't I?' She noses my hand and looks up, her eyes sorrowful. 'Neglecting me again for Janus, you are.' I've been away all of twenty minutes and in sight most of the time.

I put Janus in the car and he lies down and he heaves a deep sigh and goes off into a dream of remembering; he has had his little bit of exercise and is happy and now we have some real exercising to do, as Chita and I set off at a fast sprint into the woods, to find out whether there are deer, or strange birds or perhaps bears and lions and tigers.

Chita is never sure.

At Caernarfon Show she met Jamie the St Bernard for the first time since he has grown up. He used to come to club when he was only about a mile high. Now he is around ten miles high, to judge by Chita's expression. He leaped out of his car, enchanted by this dainty little miss, and she gave an appalled stare and we took off fast. Luckily someone fielded Jamie and his owner apologized and Chita decided, about ten minutes later, that she could relax. The lion had gone.

I hoped we would not meet any large dogs in the wood, or deer. I'd no desire to suffer a dislocated shoulder as Chita fled.

She saw Joy on the other track and called out to her. Joy didn't hear her, so we took off and I had to be very firm indeed. 'Behave, little madam.' We heeled like ladies down the drive, but when she finally met Joy she went wild.

Chita going wild has to be seen to be believed. Joy responded and we settled my small ball of fire.

At last she condescended to sit and be stroked in a civilized manner. We laughed and put Chita in the car. The two Shelties and Janus blended in colour; Chita's darkness showed up in the huddle of fur, but the dogs all behaved when we were driving. Joy is firm with her dogs and she only had to say 'down' if they grew restless and we had peace.

We drove through Yorkshire; through Ripon and through Richmond; we took little by-roads, through dales where the water rippled over grey boulders; we climbed to the tops again, some of them covered by snow. We ate at a tiny inn in the middle of nowhere; and parked the car by a stream, in the shade of a huge old tree. Snow covered the tops and clung to the trees and the countryside could not have looked more beautiful.

We walked the dogs; we drove on and we came at last to the motorway and the road home; and arrived late and very tired, to talk over our trip, to let the dogs race round the house, into the garden, up the stairs, making sure that nothing had changed in their absence.

I was to spend the rest of the week with Joy. The next day I went over to visit our son and his family who live in an old weaver's cottage. I went via the walks that we used to take when we lived there too and the dogs came out and explored; Janus remembering, I am sure. It was all new to Chita as she was born in Wales and never knew our old home.

On the Saturday I went to our daughter's and walked the dogs across the footpaths, while she and her husband laid a new carpet that timed its coming rather badly within moments of our arrival. They have a bungalow with two bedrooms leading out of one another, and I slept in the far room. The dogs decided at early dawn on Sunday that come what might, they must go outside, and we crept, startling the three cats who exploded out of the catdoor into the garden.

I couldn't go through to my room again so stayed downstairs, baffled by the gas fire which has the most peculiar switch, without book or glasses to read with, sitting and thinking, for a remarkably long time as it was Sunday morning.

The snow had started again and I was afraid of being marooned so left early and halfway home realized to my dismay that I was starting a dose of 'flu.

'Flu with Chita is a hazard, as it was with Puma. Puma wouldn't even eat if I weren't there and had to be fed by my bed; she wouldn't go into the garden unless I was there so that I huddled into my clothes and stood by the door and she did go out. Chita decided she couldn't stand life with me not there.

Every time the door was opened she raced upstairs, which is not allowed, to lie between my bed and the window, obviously hoping she couldn't be seen.

Kenneth had to call and call to get her downstairs.

All in all, it's much better not to be ill with a dog like Chita around.

Chapter Eleven

I finished *Three's A Pack* on a note of hope; who could tell what the future would bring? I included letters from friends and a report from Edith who had been training us. This time I include letters from other people, who have only met Chita since she improved in behaviour and never knew her when she was a real headache, when I often felt despair, especially when she was criticized by those who know little about dogs, having confined themselves to one or two easy little dogs. Large dogs need very different handling.

You can pick up a small dog spoiling for a fight. You have to control a large dog; there is no way a small woman can lift a fifty-pound struggling animal off the ground and prevent him causing a riot! He must learn to obey.

So Chita had to be controlled, come what may, just as every other large dog must be controlled. This meant studying many methods of training dogs, including those used for problem dogs. It meant hours with Bob and Edith and one day, out of those hours, a new idea was born.

It was an idea I had had for some time but I had not worked out how to implement it, as now much of my time is taken up by answering letters from people who do have dogs like mine and need help. (And please, I love letters, but even 10 letters second-class cost well over £1, and we do need postage if we are to reply.) The same plan had been in Edith and Bob's minds – and together it was possible.

I had been on a number of Edith's courses; and was learning all the time; and still need to go on learning, as we all do, because there is always something new to know. So out of both our ideas the Garreg Ddu Canine Education Centre was born; to help pet owners with major dog problems. The dogs can come, or the owners come with the dogs (which is far better) and they are taught what to do; the results are very rewarding as there is nothing more satisfying than to see a dog that came to club, or to Edith, out-of-hand, and watch a happy owner go off with a relaxed dog that understands now how it is supposed to behave. It is only a matter of teaching the owner what to do; dog training is a skill, and so few people realize it, expecting to learn in a few minutes every week something that has taken someone else years of practice to perfect.

Also it is sometimes easier if the large dogs are first trained by men as few women have the necessary physical strength to manage a powerful year-old German Shepherd, even if he has no behaviour problems other than those of youth.

So with the Centre in mind I enrolled on Edith's and Bob's Instructors' Course with the idea of getting my Advanced Instructors' Certificate before I finished this book and before we started on the Education Centre properly, as it is the holiday season and impossible to get around in a tourist area. It takes me double the time to get to Edith's home, forty miles away, where we work, as she has space and equipment.

The Course was again in the Bangor Normal College which is a splendid venue; with room to work in, facilities for making tea and coffee, residential for those who need it and very good meals provided by well-qualified and thoughtful staff.

The work, as I expected, was gruelling. It involved practice taking classes; how many ways there are of putting dogs into a down position when they have never been taught; easy dogs, difficult dogs, large dogs, small dogs, problem dogs, different breeds. They all differ and since no two dogs are alike what works for one may not for another; you have to find out.

There were a number of unusual breeds: a Hungarian Vislar; a Great Munsterlander; a Giant Schnauzer; a Turverren, a Groenendahl, a Malinois; there were small dogs, one of them a King Charles Cavalier spaniel that is beautifully trained; and large dogs; and handlers of all ages. I was one of the oldest there; which can be funny as younger generations tend to think Grandma is past it.

We worked for four days; morning, afternoon and evening. Our new video equipment for the Centre was a boon as it is easier to watch things done than to listen to how they are done; and mistakes can be pointed out when seen on the screen, as inexperienced handlers helped make the films. These are all made by Bob, with Edith revealing rather remarkable hidden acting qualities at times as she shows us the sort of instructor we should not be: lacking knowledge, careless, badly dressed in dirty clothes and yelling at the class and the dogs. It was a very funny performance providing both instruction and light relief after a hard day out of doors.

Though August, we had the usual patchy weather and plenty of rain. Nice for my farm neighbours; lovely bit of rain, swell the peas, it will, they say, beaming as I splash with dogs through the puddles. I had to be up early to exercise both dogs before classes began as I commuted from home.

By the end of the week I knew I was going to fail. And I very badly wanted to pass as I felt that I would also fail Edith and Bob who had taken so much time teaching me both in the past and now. Also I wanted to be better qualified as I run the local dog club and it's always better to have the ability to instruct better than before; it is a continuing process; and hopefully you can achieve far more with more knowledge.

I drove home each evening and reviewed the day's work and slowly my confidence ebbed away. I wasn't the only one losing heart; four of the six of us who had decided to apply for our Advanced Certificates changed our minds. No way were we going to pass. We would try to get a better Instructor's Certificate. Two of the men were almost as old as me, and they also joined me in changing their minds.

We struggled on.

There was a written exam which wasn't too bad. There was also an oral and just before this I had got into a mild argument about certain competition rules; I had known them well, but the last thing I remembered was someone who had contradicted me; I repeated what she had said . . . and got it wrong. I knew as soon as I shut the door afterwards I had been right in the first place, but too late now.

Oh, well, and now for the practical tomorrow.

I have a very soft voice, as a rule; or at least, I did BC (which in our house means Before Chita). So up I got, early, and went out into the woods; all alone and nobody there, or so I thought until I saw a man watching me.

And as I drove back to the college to take my practical, I came up with a silly piece of doggerel about my rehearsal there alone in the woods.

If you go down in the woods today, you had better take a gun.
There's a woman down in the woods today having the oddest fun.
She's standing there beneath the trees, talking to dogs that nobody sees,
Saying, 'Susan, watch your pup!' Dial 999 and lock her up!

I'd been rehearsing voice control with an imaginary class, sure no one would be there before 8.00 a.m.!

A little later, having time to kill, as I was last, which was steadily demoralizing me as one after another came out in despair and talked about the awful mistakes they had made, I took Chita for a walk and went down to the football pitch. It was 3.00 p.m. and no way would I be taking my exam till 5.00; my confidence had dropped into my boots. I walked on the pitch knowing I would probably produce a pathetic squeak, or a whimper, something like Chita produces when I tell her to 'speak'. I knew just how she feels.

So, pretending I was taking a poetry exam, I stood in the middle of what I thought was an empty field declaiming 'The Way Through the Woods'. And discovered my voice did carry, as interested people on the road above stared down at this idiot woman talking away to nobody.

Where can one go to rehearse?

Even my own field has fishermen beyond it; and in the house Kenneth is likely to say 'Are you all right?' as I practise my voice control; while Liz looks a little anxious as she rushes round doing all the housework for me and doing it far better than I can. I couldn't live and write without Liz.

Then came the final dinner; my morale dropped even lower as I changed. It plummeted to the depths when the lock of the bathroom I had borrowed jammed and I had visions of being there for ever! The meal was very good, though I suspect we were all rather on edge, and conversation was stilted and not as free-flowing as usual, as everyone was in a nail-biting mood. I had helped wash teacups on the last two days as both times I was last; and had also emptied ashtrays: I have never seen ashtrays so full and we felt we ought to have a letter of thanks from the revenue collectors. I don't smoke, but even I felt the need for one cigarette and gave up smoking again at the end of the course.

Results came; those who had not gained the necessary marks for an Instructor's Certificate came first; we waited, holding our breath. Then came those who had gained the required 75% for their Instructor's Certificates which are very handsome indeed. Our judge was Muriel Pearce, who has had five champions and won Cruft's five times and is a gorgeous person but in those circumstances is a very daunting examiner as she knows so much more than we do; no way would I teach if she visited my club; I would hand over to her. Here was I only two hours before taking a class in front of her and in total panic, which she commented on later; I left out two things I knew extremely well and totally forgot to mention, and knew I had lost marks.

Then came those who had passed their Advanced; only four of us and I was third with 89½% which is a result I will cherish for ever, as younger people tend to think the older members of the community well past it! In fact we have the experience they lack as we have so many more years of dog owning and dog watching to draw on if asked an awkward question. There was that dog in 1969 . . . or even further back than that, or the dog in our childhood, of a breed no one sees today; now that method that worked on him would work here.

The courses help to pass on experience; nobody acquires enough. I know a police sergeant in charge of dog training who once commented that the more he learned the less he felt he knew; there is so much to grasp, so much more to understand and many of the books on the subject skim the surface and are not always right either.

So now I had my Advanced Instructors' Certificate and could take my place as Edith's partner without feeling I had too little qualification; which does not mean I now know it all; it means I have a broader basis on which to begin to start learning much more than I now know. I had to answer one question in my oral on ways of curing a dog that lags.

I have spent ten years with a dog that lags as retrievers often do; and my answer was pretty comprehensive, so that Muriel commented that I had mentioned some things she had never heard of; and she is very much better qualified than I am.

We can all teach each other all the time, in every field.

John, who was top with 98%, was like an encyclopaedia of dog knowledge and I wished I lived nearer to him to enable us to discuss dogs at times. He knew so many ways of doing everything.

Chapter Twelve

I had now achieved two ambitions. I have my Advanced Certificate and we have founded the Education Centre. Now for the next stage.

I have now had four years of teaching Chita; four years in which I have been helped by three police-dog sergeants and a retired inspector on the police-dog section who I can write to or 'phone if I have a tracking or searching problem; four years during which she has competed in four CD stakes and two UD stakes and several Obedience shows. One Trials in particular comes to my mind, when she went into a blind panic on her downstay. This is ten minutes with me out of sight and Chita hates me being out of sight.

I went out of sight and she came too, at once, which is not the general idea. The judge suggested that I should put her down with the next group and he would get his wife to hold her to prove to her that she must stay on the spot when I went out of her view. I came back to find him trying to hold Chita, saying 'I've never met a dog like yours. You *do* have a problem.' Chita almost broke the lead in her struggles.

John Grantham was an extremely nice judge to have and was very kind, and very concerned, instead of criticizing and condemning as one or two will do. I was very grateful to him for his help and every time we met again he asked how we were doing.

He has had a lot of experience with his own dogs.

Roy Hunter has been fascinated by Chita from the first and thought her smashing. His comment when he saw her was 'What a *challenge*. Aren't you *lucky*?' At that stage I wasn't yet quite sure I was lucky; she certainly always is a challenge, though now she is a relaxed challenge with her own idiotic sense of humour. Little zany! Maybe we never will qualify but she will have taught me far more than any easy dog and taken me into realms I would never have ventured into had I had an easy dog. It wouldn't have been necessary and I would never have known of further training, and would not have met Edith. I owe so much to having this one special dog.

You never know where life will lead you. I spent my war years in Wales, as our college was evacuated. All those years ago I thought I would never return. Yet here I am, a grandmother, leading a far more full and active life than I did then, spending my time, as I once hoped to, with dogs and with those who have dogs that need training, and often quietly amused by people much younger who seem unaware that being older these days does not mean being either inactive or senile; it takes a very long time now to age, and even at ninety my two aunts are capable of far more intelligent conversation about world affairs than many people half their age.

Chita has taken years off my life, as she made me decide at last to lose weight. I joined Weight Watchers, and lost over twenty pounds in a year, which in turn helped me to train her better as I found moving around much easier and far more fun; the arthritic pains I had had cleared up, again with help from someone I value very much in my life; a day's work is no longer daunting but something to look forward to, and like my dog I wonder eagerly what today will bring.

What today brought was Roy's evaluation of Chita, together with the story of his own training life, to authenticate what he said. Like many police-dog instructors he has wide experience of dogs, and also of dog nature, of dog behaviour and obviously a long-standing knowledge of the GSD under training conditions, something which breeders will never see and most owners also will never know.

A police-dog is a very exceptional animal. Few people realize how exceptional as it must stand up to the kind of stress most humans never endure. Riots and football crowds, mobs and violence, guns and sticks and attacks of varying forms, which few of us hear about. Violent men who are arrested don't come quietly with pleasant manners; they fight and the policeman can be unfairly criticized for defending himself, though if you or I had to face up to that attack and did defend ourselves, it would immediately be acknowledged as self-defence, and we would probably be congratulated for our courage. Life isn't fair!

A growling dog under control can make an immense difference. I once took a Special Constables' course. One night four youths burgled a building, broke a policeman's nose and put up a considerable fight before the dog handlers arrived. (I was in the police station when they returned. Our class had just ended and I was about to drive home.)

Two dogs that could be made to appear savage and also if necessary be allowed to attack, changed the situation entirely. All I saw was four very obviously frightened youths walking quietly, shepherded by dogs that growled if they moved in the wrong direction while the police handlers with them supervised the procession. The dogs did not touch the youths; the men did not touch them; they came into the station as meekly as any youth could do, and though there had been a considerable fight to resist arrest in the first place, now everything was calm and under control.

It reminded me of another night when a police-dog would have been very useful. I went out on night patrol with a serving officer and a special constable. We passed an old peoples' home in the process of construction and saw four figures duck down out of sight.

The car was stopped, everyone got out and the policeman called to us 'Head them off'. I started to, met one of them who looked about nine feet high and was carrying a stick and I ducked back into the car, not being trained in unarmed combat, and not being on duty either, and at a considerable disadvantage at five feet tall. The special constable, who was well over fifty, and on his first night out, came back, having been unable to run fast enough and was very out of breath indeed. I hoped he wouldn't have a heart attack as it was before the days of radio cars and also before personal radio, so no help could be called fast.

The police officer came back, having failed to catch any of them, and we took torches to see what they had done. One newly concreted floor was covered in heel-marks and toe-marks, which must have taken hours of savage delight to make; and the rest of the place was flooded as they had turned on all the taps to the hoses.

The damage was immense and the culprits weren't caught. A dog would have caught at least one of them. I would also have felt much safer with a dog beside me. There is nothing like a well-trained guarding German Shepherd to give you confidence.

I wrote *Walk a Lonely Road* soon after that and asked how I could thank the police for all the help they had given me. They were immensely helpful, correcting what I wrote, from the point of view of police procedure; bringing the dogs over to show me how they were trained and how they were worked; taking me tracking and showing me training films which showed the dogs in action, on searches, on simulated incidents, and on a variety of police work, such as looking for old people who have wandered away, or lost children. The police do not only deal with criminals. Lose a child or indeed any older person, and you have teams of very concerned and dedicated men who are determined to find that child as fast as possible.

It was suggested that I present a cup for the best teamwork each year involving a serving dog-handler and his dog. This has usually gone to someone who has produced a painstaking effort and had perhaps one of the duller jobs of police work that is very necessary but never hits the headlines. It has been well worth-while. The real problem is that the cup is difficult to award as everyone has had the same type of work to do; and everyone has also had success. Each man could well be rewarded.

So the Avenger Cup was duly presented, and every year since 1969 I have been over to give it in person, and spent two days with the dog handlers, watching the Police Dog Trials; watching the dogs track, search, talking to the various handlers, watching the criminal work, which is fascinating as the dogs have to chase after 'criminals' armed with guns or sticks and if the man surrenders, then the dog is stopped in mid-chase and told to stand still and bark, or to circle the man and bark, depending on how close he got in the first place.

The dogs search buildings, and can find drugs even when extremely well hidden. Any dog can be trained to find lost articles; Chita is good at it and could be taken on to train for drug finding or explosives finding, given the right instructor. A police-dog instructor has to cover a wide range of fields and have immense knowledge, and I think that few of those who do not deal with dogs realize how demanding this area of training can be.

Not only the dog must be trained, the man needs training too. Many of us who train in clubs and teach others in clubs know how difficult it is for someone who has never had a dog before to appreciate at first that the dog does not think like a human, but has a mind of its own; and also a way of thinking all its own. Until we understand how our dogs think, we won't make progress.

So that it was with considerable eagerness that I read Roy's assessment, hoping he hadn't thought my part of the team too inadequate. Edith's comments in *Three's A Pack* were not exactly flattering!

Roy started by giving his own experience for the sake of readers who won't know the background of men like him. His experience as a dog handler began in 1958, when he was a police constable in the Metropolitan police dog section; he then became a sergeant instructor, holding a Home Office police-dog instructor's certificate, which had to be worked for. He was promoted to station sergeant and at one time was Deputy Chief Instructor, still in the Metropolitan police force.

He became an inspector and was Area Dog Officer in charge of five sergeants and eighty police dog handlers until 1980 when he retired, so that his experience is very comprehensive.

Like all those of us who are interested in instructing others, and also very interested in dogs generally (which does not always apply) he has attended a number of courses; at the Search and Rescue Dog Centre in Scotland in 1973, where he qualified a Rottweiler; he also attended the Sieger (Schutzhund) Dog Trials as a spectator in Germany in 1978, 1979 and 1980. The Sieger qualifications in Germany are for man-work among the other attributes and the dogs are thoroughly tested in a way that we do not do here, though many of us would like to see something like it introduced as it does sort out temperament; only bold dogs with courage and also dogs that are eminently trainable are of use in any form of higher training.

Nervous dogs can be trained and used very successfully but that is a slow process and needs the right person and a vast amount of time; no serving officer could spend the time needed to produce good results from a dog like Chita, for instance. She would have been turned down on that count alone, as her fear of other dogs when she was young would have been a major handicap. She attacked through fear and she still is very wary of dogs that snarl at her, though she would not dream of attacking them now. Her attitude then was 'I'll get you before you get me,' which can also be a human attitude with aggressive people who feel inferior.

Roy also visited the German War Dog School in 1979–80 and the German Customs Dog School in 1980. He was awarded an Advanced Instructor's certificate at the British Institute of Professional Dog Handlers (Obedience division) in 1978.

I have included those details for another reason, which is to show how much extra time a good instructor had to put in, as there is always something more to learn about dogs. You would think that after retiring in 1980 he might have a change, but not a bit of it, as he has started a dog club in his own village, and he attended the Point Volhard Obedience Instructors' Course at Syracuse, USA in 1980, and the Volhard-Laird Course in Virginia, USA in 1981. The Volhards are among the most dedicated of instructors in the USA where they take the need for good instructors to a much further degree than we do here.

There are courses in England for would-be instructors; Norman Hill's at Totnes, and the British Institute at Hatfield; and Edith Nicholls now runs one in Wales, where Garreg Ddu courses insist on qualification at a very high level; those coming do not necessarily qualify. Nor do they on the others. I have been to Totnes twice and have two certificates from there.

Roy went on to attend a seminar by Johan Greaves on Schutzhund training in the USA. He also had his own dog Abelard, a Rottweiler, that he qualified in civilian Working Trials as TD (Tracker Dog) excellent, when he was only two years and two weeks old (the dog, not Roy!)

Apart from his police dog instructing he has given a number of courses for civilian handlers for Working Trials, and has taught 265 handlers, which included those on a course he gave in the USA, he has instructed many more for Obedience, and he has also run civilian dog clubs.

Those of us lucky enough to have an interested police-dog handler near who will give his time are always extremely grateful though maybe we don't say so often enough! Roy's courses are in great demand; he gave one here, for just one day, and I went on one of his longer courses for beginner handlers in Working Trials and found it extremely helpful. I was lucky enough to be able to pick his brains and get help with tracking when he and Lois stayed with us this summer. Unluckily the weather was pretty vile and the day of his course was so windy it was all we could do to stand up at times and the smaller dogs were nearly blown over.

We hope he will give a longer course here next year. I haven't asked him yet!

This is what Roy writes:

I first met Chita in April 1980. She was then two and a half years old, but her character was well developed. And how!

I think if people like Joyce and others with hyperactive dogs persevere and get some measure of success, then they have proved *they* can train dogs, and should hold their heads high, though they never attain the dizzy heights. (I hope that will cheer some of you who wrote to me in despair – JS)

Chita certainly is hyperactive. I remarked at the time that she was like a coiled spring, a bundle of energy. The downstay was non-existent and Joyce only had to go near the jumps for Chita to take off without any command, over and back!

At the end of the weekend there was a slight improvement. A full weekend of trials training is very tiring to all dogs and this combined with Joyce's perseverance enabled her to walk past the jumps without the immediate reaction from Chita. The downstay also improved but Joyce had to be in sight.

I never once saw the dog attack another dog or person.

I next saw Joyce when she asked me to give a talk to four Obedience clubs in North Wales in 1980. We had some time to spare so I asked her if I could handle the little bitch. She walked quietly to heel most of the time, but with that expression in her eyes which says 'just you relax for one minute and then we'll see!' On the way back to Joyce Chita took me by surprise with her strength as she lunged and I was towed back to Joyce.

The last time I had the pleasure (and I mean that) of meeting this extrovert little dog was in June this year when I took a one day CD course on Anglesey. Chita, while still being a ball of energy was more under Joyce's control and this day did her out of sight downstay.

It might take some time for Joyce to get the dog to do her stays in a Trials environment. However I am sure with her tenacity Joyce will eventually get CD and UD. I know that when she does it won't go to her head; she will just carry on quietly writing books, training her own dogs and helping other people in her area with their dogs and puppies at the dog club she runs in North Wales.

It will be nice to see a book one day titled *Success with Chita.*

(signed) Roy Hunter

Since Roy has a genius for making somewhat tactless remarks at times, (like me he's a Cockney and we aren't renowned for diplomacy) especially about one's dog handling, or even perhaps one's voice or one's weight, he does not mince his words and no way would he have given me anything to put in my book that he hadn't felt sincerely; so I did feel rather relieved when I finished reading what he wrote. I would still have included it if it had been unfavourable; as I did Edith's criticism of me in *Three's A Pack*; I didn't shine when she first met me in any way at all, when Chita was a year old, but Roy does know about dogs and, like Edith, reassured me, knowing it was the dog that was causing problems to me, as only an expert could possibly help me to learn to handle her.

Perhaps here is as good a place as any to say what is needed in Trials. The lowest stake, the Companion Dog (CD) has four sections. The Obedience section consists of the control section, which includes heel on the lead, heel free, calling the dog to the handler, which is a formal exercise and has several parts all of which must be done correctly without the dog anticipating or refusing, and then the dog has to be sent away from the handler in a straight line to a point (which may be invisible) directed by the judge for a distance of twenty yards. This exercise is remarkably difficult to teach and takes ages to do so properly. It is very easy to teach it wrong and get the oddest results in consequence. For this section the handler gets one hundred marks and needs 80% to qualify 'excellent', 70% qualifies. In an Open Trial it is necessary to get 80% to qualify for Championship Trials in the CD, UD, and TD stakes.

The 'stays' consist of the dog sitting without moving for two minutes with the handler out of sight, and staying still until told to move when he returns, and then lying down for ten minutes without moving with the handler out of sight. All handlers who have done this exercise will agree that those ten minutes take about an hour to pass at least! The dog has to get 100% on these two exercises or you can't qualify at all and with a dog like Chita I can get 100% if she is good enough in all other exercises, yet if she moves in this I still can't qualify her at all, as this is the hardest of all for her type of dog. She hates lying still and she hates me out of her sight. Some dogs don't mind.

The agility consists of a six-foot upright scale; the dog must go over, stay out of sight and come back only when told; a three-foot hurdle and a nine-foot long-jump.

The search is for three objects in a fifteen-yard square; the dog has to go in alone; the handler must stay outside and direct the dog from a distance. The articles are small; like cartridge cases, and the dog has to find them by human scent, which is not the handler's scent, but that of the search steward, who the dog has usually never met before.

Then the dog has to go out and fetch back its dumbbell, which is thrown for as far as the handler can manage as a rule in Trials.

That is the elementary stake!

The Utility Dog (UD) stake has a longer sendaway, of fifty yards; and also the dog must not panic if a gun is fired, but be quite steady. The search area is twenty-five yards square (the squares are marked by corner poles, and may be grass, wheat, heather, bracken, etc.) and contain four articles this time.

Also the dog must follow a track laid by a total

stranger half an hour before the dog is asked to find it. The track is half a mile long, and has on it one article, at the end; and may have a number of corners so that it can zigzag. It may be on grass, woodland, forest, plough, or stubble.

And it is far from easy to train a dog to this standard. Many people try; many people fail to qualify.

The Working Dog (WD) stake is similar, but the track is laid one and a half hours before the dog has to nose it out, and two articles are laid on it. In all cases you must get 80% overall for 'excellent' and 70% to qualify; in the UD and WD stakes there are 200 marks, most of them for the track and search so it is not possible to qualify unless your dog can do both well.

The Tracker Dog (TD) stake has a change in the sendaway. The dog is sent out fifty yards and then has to be re-directed to the right or the left as the judge asks. There are three articles on the track and the track is laid three hours before the dog works it.

Also in this stake there is one extra exercise; the dog must 'speak' on command.

All these exercises are part of police-dog work but only dogs trained for man-work go on to the PD (Police Dog) stake. The first three parts of this are exactly like the Tracker Dog stake, but the track need only by one and a half hours old and only two articles. The major marks in this stake go on the patrol work.

The dog has to quarter the ground (a zigzag search for a hidden 'criminal' who may be hiding behind trees, or under bushes, etc.) His courage is tested by firing a gun at him (blank cartridges, of course!); he has to search for a criminal and escort him back to the place designated (which in real life would be a police car); he has to be called off the criminal and not go in and attack; and he has to pursue and detain a running criminal.

This is the end product; the dog mustn't bark or whine constantly while he or she is working; the handlers can only give the dog certain commands; for instance in heeling the dog must be by your side but you can only say 'HEEL' as you start off; you are penalized by the judge if you tell him to walk close beside you, or to sit; he must sit when you stop without a command. The number of commands that can be given in the other exercises are also regulated.

You can't use your lead either to help the dog. The dog really does have to be trained to a very high degree even for the lower stakes.

A lot of people just starting in the dog competition world come in to Trials to 'have a go'. While you can do this in Obedience, I personally don't think it wise in Trials as one of the greatest requirements in training dogs is that you never set them tasks beyond their ability, or they become depressed, lose confidence and won't try again. After all, if we are repeatedly told to play Beethoven sonatas when we have not yet learned the five-finger exercises we are going to come to grief and a lot of Obedience people are doing this to their dogs without knowing they are.

Even the Companion Dog stake is higher than beginner and novice Obedience. The heelwork without-out commands is only done in Obedience in higher classes when the dog understands the elementary work; no sensible person would try and work a young dog in the top class; he isn't up to it. He needs chatting up to give him confidence. You can do this in the lower classes, not later on.

The agility work needs training carefully, or dogs end up lame.

The dog also needs to be fed well, exercised well and be very fit as it is very demanding for him to do this amount of work on one day and nowadays he may be asked to take two stakes the same day and do everything twice. It is possible to take both the Companion Dog stake and the Utility Dog stake the same day at the same Trials and it's a lot of stress and work for the dog, especially in strange places after long journeys as Trials are few and far between.

The stays are those of the higher classes in competition and it is daft to expect a dog that has done a two-minute downstay with the handler in sight to suddenly be asked to do a ten-minute downstay with the handler out of sight. He has never met the situation before and is probably convinced he has been deserted.

We don't normally leave our dogs on their own with lots of other dogs and then disappear. They need to be given confidence and the exercise must be built up gradually.

So many of the exercises are long-term to teach; the sendaway, if it is to be sound; the tracking, which can be mucked up as we don't know what dogs smell; the dog can be made gunshy if he has never heard a gun until his first Trials

At one Trials nine dogs were lined up in the sit position, we were told to take four paces away from them, the gun was fired, and four dogs bolted. Chita did sit like a rock. 'Silly noise,' she said with her eyes. 'What did he do that for?' People here do shoot often across the river, as the farmer opposite lets his shooting, and we have pheasants the way townsfolk have sparrows and don't think much about them unless they pull up the peas and the onions, which they delight in doing.

Trials is better than Obedience, in my opinion, for the hyperactive dog, as it gives it far more to think about. Chita is much more tired after an afternoon spent practising track search, sendaway and downstay than she is after a long romp in the woods or along the beach, where she plays the fool, doesn't use her wits, and gees herself up, and is vastly refreshed. It does nothing to tire her in any way.

Pups are better given fun games that lead on to Trials than allowed to rush around, eat anything in sight, and come in and be sick, bringing up grass, dead leaves, coke, stones and what have you, having been allowed to run riot instead of being carefully played with with a view to bringing them up sensibly. Children that run riot end up being part of riots in inner cities. Dogs that run riot end up part of a killing pack; they won't stay at home as they have been given the taste of too much freedom; they don't need to rush about like idiots for exercise any more than we do. If we exercise we get more benefit from controlled and disciplined games like tennis, badminton, golf, all of which use our skills, and in which we can improve.

It's fun if you take it the right way and it is very, very rewarding to see the wild puppy come under control, obey your commands, wait for you to tell him what you want done next and not 'argue' with you.

Dogs often train their owners; out when dog wants, eat when dog wants, up when dog wants, dog rushing like a maniac round the house, dog wanting to play all evening; if dog has had his exercise which you give him rather than turn him out to do his own thing, and if dog has had his food and sufficient use of his brain, then dog learns to lie quietly until you tell him it is time for some interest in his life. Obviously he has fun during the evening. I hide things for Chita to find. It's a lovely game for her, and exercises her mind.

Chita loves training. She has responded in a way that fascinates me and also fascinates those who know her well. She has a distant relative at club – Lady – who is like Chita. There are others who meet her, some daily, some weekly, and they too have a part in this book, as through them I have had a great deal of help; from Lesley Savage who lays my tracks for me (something that needs doing with great care or the dog will fail because of human error); from Edith and Bob who have become fascinated by Chita's training, so that together we hope to produce results that I could not produce alone as every handler needs someone to watch and point out mistakes; it's so easy to turn wrong, to step into your dog, to walk too fast or too slowly, to make a botched signal, and it is easier to correct someone else than to correct yourself. You can't walk behind yourself at your own side and you can't see what the back end of the dog is doing as you walk along by its head! Even a Cruft's winner is the result of a team effort and so much depends on the person who trained the winners – perhaps more – than on the winners.

Chapter Thirteen

Now that Chita is being trained for tracking and searching, for all the additional exercises in Working Trials, she is also discovering that life has meaning for her. She knows that when we meet another dog she sits by my side and never rushes at it; she knows that when we cross the road she sits at the kerb and waits till the road is clear; she knows that when I am writing she takes her place in her favourite spot, near the door, ready to warn me of the telephone, the doorbell or of something unexpected by both of us.

She is learning, slowly, because she is a very enthusiastic, happy dog, that when friends call she doesn't leap to lick their faces but sits still to be stroked and greeted sensibly; although that has always been difficult for her, as she so wants to tell our friends how much she loves them; and they of course, for the most part, are delighted to be told.

There are now a number of people who, as well as Roy Hunter and Pat O'Shea and Ron Tribe, have had the chance to know Chita well, as she comes to dog club, or we track together and sometimes work together, and it is always fascinating to see a dog through other peoples' eyes.

Sally first came to club last year with her Boxer, Susie. She had moved to the area from Harlech and had been a member of Edith's club, so that she already knows a good deal about dog training and is now able to help new members with their dogs at club. Susie is still young, an enthusiast in her own way, with the Boxer knack of wriggling her whole body in delight when she meets her friends. If I don't talk to Susie, she feels her evening has been lacking, and it always amuses me when I go over to her, as there is no dog that manages to welcome you in quite the way a Boxer does; it may be something to do with having no tail;

Susie has to wag everything.

She is learning to retrieve now, another skill that is difficult to teach most dogs, and the Terriers and Boxers most of all as they don't do it naturally, though most dogs will play with their mouths and carry things, so it ought to be possible. Nearly all bitches carry their pups at times.

This is what Sally wrote of Chita:

I have known both Joyce and Chita for over a year now, and both have made a deep and lasting impression on my life. Joyce, by her kindness to me, and her complete dedication to all dogs, whatever breed, size or temperament. Chita by the sheer weight of her personality.

Chita and I have formed a relationship, which I find most endearing. Her favourite expression of affection to me, is to gently nibble my ear, snuffling into my hair, whilst quietly crooning in the back of her throat. Chita adores people, she loves company, she is an extrovert, who will do all in her power to gain your attention, and having achieved that attention, will give all the love and affection she can muster.

Chita is one of the most intelligent dogs I have ever encountered, and that intelligence Joyce has directed and developed by her most careful and thoughtful training. Without this channelling, without this outlet for her intelligence, Chita would have been a very different, and probably difficult animal. Therefore, all credit must go to Joyce, who through her careful observation, and analysis of Chita, has now achieved a unique, and splendid companion for life.

(signed) Sally Clark,
devoted admirer and friend of Chita.

Lesley is my tracking companion. Rudi, the Dobermann, is just beginning to track; he is only a year old, and like many of our dogs now, he joined the club when he was twelve weeks old, so that Lesley, when she found out I was short of tracking ground, very soon discovered her farmer neighbour would let us use the fields just beyond her cottage.

Sometimes Lesley laid tracks for me; sometimes I went up to the field and worked alone; and on icy winter days she would call from the window to come and get warm with a cup of coffee, which was extremely welcome as winter last year was bleak and bitter here with searing winds that never seemed to stop.

Wind is a major part of our lives near the sea; gales in the Irish Sea mean not only that the trees are tossing wildly, and the sky is full of scudding clouds but I have a little bitch that has gone wind crazy and can't think properly, as she never behaves normally on windy days or when the moon is full.

Children can be affected too so that teachers dread wind, as every child is affected by it and those that are normally excitable are much more so. Chita finds the wind very exciting; it leads her still to disobey, to race wildly if she is free instead of coming to heel, to whip over the jumps instead of doing as she has been told and when she was a tiny pup, on windy days and on moony nights she would race in circles, like a little wrongly shaped greyhound, so fast that she was impossible to stop, to catch or to distract.

That kind of behaviour is behind her now, but wind still presents problems and I always hope that if we are competing anywhere that the wind will not strengthen to a blustery gale, as then I have to exert all my authority over her to get any sense out of her at all.

Also that wind madness can be dangerous to the dog, as she can run into danger, racing towards a road where a car may kill or injure her badly. At the vet's I have seen the results of too many road accidents to be happy about that.

Lesley, writing about Chita, commented as everyone does, on her immense strength. If Chita pits her physical strength against anyone, she does create problems as they can't hold her or check her; she comes to me:

I first saw Chita as a three-year-old, behaving beautifully, demonstrating what could be achieved with our unruly puppies. It was our first night at dog club with our Dobermann pup, just twelve weeks old, and after an hour of cooing, cajoling and bribing him through the basics, it gave us real hope to see Chita's performance.

I hadn't realized just what problems Joyce had had in those early days; any lesser being would have given up after a month, I know I would have. I've never seen such an energetic, enthusiastic dog, she wears me out just watching her hurtle from one exercise to another, a four-legged power-pack, radiating her happiness at being on the go.

For one little dog she is immensely strong, as I found out the day Joyce asked me to fetch her from the car. All went well until she saw her Mum and it was all I could do to stay upright. Being dragged towards Joyce was a bit like riding a horse that's got the bit between the teeth, and it was impossible to gain any slack in the lead to correct her.

To someone like Joyce, with an abundance of patience and determination, Chita must be very rewarding.

(signed) Lesley Savage

Sandra joined our dog club last year. She came in with two German Shepherds; Lady, who is bigger than Chita, light in colour, and has a very hard streak in her; and Lady's daughter, Meg, who is as unlike her mother as any pup could be, and very gentle indeed; almost too gentle, although last night for some unknown reason known only to Meg, she played the fool, doing, for the most part, exactly the opposite of what she was told.

Lady made herself memorable by her behaviour in the first few weeks, as she came in reminding me of Chita at her worst, and decided no other dog was going to come near her owner; she'd see them off, and she did. She nipped them.

Sandra found dog night tough going, as she had her

two children to watch as well as four dogs, but the two girls do as they are told and are very co-operative, so don't normally cause us any problems, though like all youngsters they can have their moments!

Meanwhile Sandra's problems with Lady continued, though she never showed Chita's early wild aggression to other dogs. Lady was sneaky. I saw a lot of the problems I had had with Chita coming to the fore, but there never seemed to be time to talk in club as there are always a number of owners with problems. Lady I did want to see progress, and I did want to somehow show Sandra I knew what she was up against, as I had a feeling when I talked to her that at other clubs she had perhaps met with a lack of sympathy and understanding. You need to have had a difficult dog yourself before you really do understand what those of us with unusually intelligent dogs have to battle with. Those who have only had easy dogs can't begin to imagine what life is like when the dog you own and the dog you are far too fond of to get rid of, is one that is constantly playing up and has a mind of its own and needs watching and more training than the easy dog before it is biddable.

Then Sandra borrowed *Three's A Pack*, and when she brought it back we luckily had a very quiet night with very few dogs and began to talk in more detail about Lady, as her owner realized I did understand her problems, and that I had had to overcome many of them myself with Chita.

I asked Sandra if she would like to write a little about Lady. I like Lady very much; we get on extremely well; she has a sense of humour that reminds me of Puma's, and when she is in the mood is an imp, full of fun. Other nights she can be full of something quite different. Last night, after her season and three weeks off, she was delighted to be back and behaved admirably. Dogs are not machines; one is never quite sure what they will do at any one time and maybe many people expect far too much of them and far too much consistency. We have our moods too.

Sandra wrote her contribution for me and when I

217

read it I realized she had been to a club at first where Lady had been under suspicion because people didn't really like the breed. Sandra was told it was absurd to get a dog of her breed for a family dog.

I know a great many Alsatians that make splendid family dogs. One of our club dogs, Lordy, lives with a baby boy and is the best companion the child could have, a huge, gentle, very faithful dog. You do, however, have to be careful where you get your dog, as Lordy's predecessor, who was related to Chita, had to go to the police. He is a wonderful police-dog, but he could not have lived with a baby; he was much too boisterous, and much too energetic. He needs a great deal of exercise and to use his brain.

Sandra, writing of Lady, says:

At dog school Lady was marvellous, very quick to learn and a great show off, but at home she was hard work, always full of energy, pull, pull, pull, lunging at other dogs, and if anyone was afraid of her she knew it and traded on it, with a curl of her top lip and a sort of growl. And how she'd whine in the car when I was going out.

Meeting Joyce and Chita, I began to compare Lady with Chita. They aren't really alike but whenever I watched Chita I could see a likeness in their temperament, though Chita never lunged or nipped. It was only when I read *Three's A Pack* that I saw a lot of problems I had had with Lady were the same, except that Lady wanted to please me from the beginning. [Lady's ideas of pleasing her owner are sometimes as odd as Chita's! J.S.]

Lady just had too much energy. On checking her pedigree we found Lady and Chita had two very dominant ancestors in common that are in a lot of dogs with the same kind of problems, as we now both know. I have found out that Lady is really content only when she has something to think about and if I neglect her training for any time, even a week, she tries to get on top of me. I have also found out that contrary to the suggestion made at the first training school I went to, she is marvellous with children, though she is inclined to be a bit over-protective.

(signed) Sandra Butler

Lady, like Chita, is an extremely endearing animal. Both have faults, but both Sandra and I know what they are and we both know that it is training that cures them; and it does cure them, provided the training is kept up. Dogs that aren't trained daily forget all they learn, just as I have forgotten my schoolgirl French and I couldn't tell you much about geography or history now either. I train my dog daily, and teach others all the time, so that that is a skill that I am gradually bringing to a higher standard. It is just the same with the dogs. Chita and Lady now will respond quickly to a command, and those commands can save their lives; can prevent them from being naughty, can stop them in mid-act; 'Chita, DOWN,' as she races after a cat; 'Lady, NO,' as she gets that gleam in her eye at the dog nearest to her. Chita was once checked by me when visiting a dog club that we had never been to before. We were staying with a friend.

'Don't keep checking your dog; she doesn't need it,' said someone who had never seen either of us before. I had checked her twice. What he didn't know was that each time I had removed a mouthful of white fur from her jaws as she had reached out to grab the dog in front of her and give him a nip, for reasons known only to Chita. I couldn't allow it; she had to be corrected. At that stage she was only seventeen *weeks* old. and if you allow a habit to develop it grows, instead of being stopped at the start; you end up with a dog that still nips when adult, and can nip hard and start a fight as other dogs resent it, not very surprisingly.

Chita no longer does it because I corrected her. She has forgotten all about it; it's not vice; it's just naughty pup. Mouthing isn't vice either; it's puppy play but if not stopped when pups start it, it can become a very bad habit as the play gets harder and fiercer and the dog may snap in fun and damage your hand quite badly.

Pups may nip too because you are clumsy with them and hurt them when you put them down or in the sit; people then blame the dog club and stop coming because the dog doesn't like being told what to do; but unless the dog can learn, then owners end up with dogs that gain more and more power over the family daily as the dog becomes the pack boss. You can't make him lie down; he doesn't like it; you can't eat a meal without him fussing for food so he gets it; you can't get him off your bed so he stays there; the family go out when dog wants; and life becomes bounded by the dog's ideas, and he is never told 'I want to do this; now BEHAVE,' which is what should happen.

It has to happen every time, or the dog thinks that you have relaxed and it can now change its behaviour and do as it likes again. Dogs never understand that; they trade on your inconsistency. Chita still trades on mine; if I don't insist she behaves when we have visitors, she doesn't, as they fuss her, and when fussed she gets silly and over-excited and may race around the house and break something, or knock over a small grandchild and it can't be allowed. 'Chita, BEHAVE.'

It has been heaven to go over regularly and talk with Edith and Bob as they understand what she is like; they have struggled with her. Bob's occasional training sessions with her are memorable to all of us, including Chita as she thought he would let her do all the things I won't let her do, like running out to the end of the lead when she saw a cat and barking at it. She found he would no more allow her to do it than I would, which surprised her as most people find her such a handful they give up and return her to me to cope with.

Chita has altered all our lives. Through her Edith and I came up with the idea of starting the Garreg Ddu Canine Education Centre to help pet owners with problems with their dogs. People can come for training, or ring up for advice and further help, or come on a course that is aimed at pet owners rather than competition people as the latter have a lot of help from very experienced handlers in the fields of both Obedience and Working Trials, while pet owners get left out – yet may need much more help

Pet owners in an area without a dog club are at a big disadvantage as they have no one to help them and there are many areas without clubs. Some had clubs but through anti-dog activity, which is often unfair and biased, they have lost their clubs. Admittedly some dog owners don't help nor do wandering dogs that foul the streets, so it's up to all of us to make sure our dogs are acceptable to other people and this is where training comes in. Your naughty dog learns what to do when he meets other dogs and meets people; and does as he is told. But training a dog is a skill; dogs don't think as we do. We have to work out how they think and that isn't easy as some dogs are easy and understand fast, others are not so bright and get anxious or muddled. Others still are much brighter than we are and while we are working out how to check them for one thing they have already done it and started on something quite different, so we get the correction wrong, and then trouble begins and gets worse as the dog knows how to get round us all the time.

Chita is that sort of dog. Even now I don't take her for granted and I never will; she waits till I am off guard and then leaps on the settee. I see her and she turns her head and leaps off fast. Not allowed, and she knows it, but she'll try it on.

We hope the Centre will grow in the years to come; it is a hobby activity for both of us on top of our own work. (Edith runs a boarding kennels and has a few litters from one or two bitches, though she doesn't breed in a large way; and books are my main activity.) I can write any literature needed; and we can keep our charges down to cover expenses as it isn't our main income. Unfortunately today petrol, writing paper, postage and telephone bills mount up in an alarming way so it can't be done for nothing.

I asked Edith and Bob if they would write the last report in this book on Chita, as they know more about us both than anyone. We meet to discuss the Centre, to plan our video shows and to make new video films. We take them to anyone who wants us, and can get an audience to cover our costs, and have already begun to discover that people find them interesting; later on, we want to do a few fun items as well as training items and items that I can use when I talk to audiences about my books. The dogs love being filmed and co-operate wonderfully and with our own dogs we have a fair variety, as among others Edith and Bob's latest Rough Collie pup, Tess, is only four months old and adorable, and knows it; she poses endlessly and is so apt to make us laugh we don't always get what we intended as she plays up to that.

Digger, their Australian cattle dog, is also a character and a half, with his own ideas on everything and occasionally is apt to interpret an exercise in his own way. Chita too will behave like an angel while we are rehearsing; three perfect performances, and then when she is live it goes to her head and she puts in her own actions; like going twice through the tunnel instead of running on, and jumping off the table and back again because she adores jumping. We are getting over that hurdle too!

She is a terrific character; maybe if she were an easy dog she wouldn't be half the fun!

She has given me an immense amount of new material for stories; has activated a whole education centre, and a new way of life for several of us; and who knows where she will take us next as we have now begun to train her so that she understands and responds, instead of wanting to be off playing all the time; and maybe we will have another book and another activity just through this one little bitch!

This is what Edith and Bob wrote:

Chita.
Time waits for no man – no dog either.

222

Many training hours are wasted by many people with doggy problems. This certainly does not apply to Joyce Stranger. She uses every valuable hour in order to improve Chita. Early morning, late evening, with all the usual chores that any woman has, plus her writing, goes into her daily time-table.

It is paying off. Chita is vastly improved. She is now extremely sociable and has actually worked Trials. To gain those extra points needed to win still needs more effort. Joyce is not yet satisfied and rightly so, but the improvement we see in both handler and dog is rewarding to say the least.

This intelligent little bitch is very crafty. She respects fair discipline but is always looking for ways to outwit humans. Joyce has now to learn to react faster and to 'read her dog' in order to prepare for the 1982 Working Trials.

(signed) Edith and Bob Nicholls

And who knows but that in a year or so we might come up with that book on Chita titled 'Success!' And maybe we won't! But we'll try, which is all that any human can do.

My little bitch is curled behind me, nose into her tail as it's a cold wet windy day and the lower field is flooded; a lake instead of grass. She is waiting for the rain to stop, as I am; for more training, working with me and no longer against me, so that now we enjoy every moment of our training together, and find it all great fun. But I still have to say, as I did when she was younger, 'Behave, little bitch.'

THE END

JOYCE STRANGER TITLES
AVAILABLE FROM CORGI BOOKS

WHILE EVERY EFFORT IS MADE TO KEEP PRICES LOW, IT IS SOMETIMES NECESSARY TO INCREASE PRICES AT SHORT NOTICE. CORGI BOOKS RESERVE THE RIGHT TO SHOW NEW RETAIL PRICES ON COVERS WHICH MAY DIFFER FROM THOSE PREVIOUSLY ADVERTISED IN THE TEXT OR ELSEWHERE.

THE PRICES SHOWN BELOW WERE CORRECT AT THE TIME OF GOING TO PRESS (NOVEMBER '84).

All these books are available at your book shop or newsagent, or can be ordered direct from the publisher. Just tick the titles you want and fill in the form below.

CORGI BOOKS, Cash Sales Department, P.O. Box 11, Falmouth, Cornwall.

Please send cheque or postal order, no currency.

Please allow cost of book(s) plus the following for postage and packing:

U.K. Customers—Allow 55p for the first book, 22p for the second book and 14p for each additional book ordered, to a maximum charge of £1.75.

B.F.P.O. and Eire—Allow 55p for the first book, 22p for the second book plus 14p per copy for the next seven books, thereafter 8p per book.

Overseas Customers—Allow £1.00 for the first book and 25p per copy for each additional book.

NAME (Block Letters)..

ADDRESS..

....